Flourish in
CAPTIVITY

GLORIA LONDOÑO

Flourish in

CAPTIVITY

A MEMOIR OF SURVIVAL, FORGIVENESS, AND HOPE

unbreakablelifewithglory@gmail.com

ISBN: 979-8-9896033-3-6 (paperback)
ISBN: 979-8-9896033-1-2 (ebook)
ISBN: 979-8-9896033-0-5 (hardcover)

Library of Congress Control Number: 2023923275

Ordering Information:
Special discounts are available on quantity purchases by corporations, associations, and others. For details, contact unbreakablelifewithglory@gmail.com

Publisher's Cataloging-in-Publication Data
Names: Londoño, Gloria, 1972- .
Title: Flourish in captivity : a memoir of survival, forgiveness, and hope / Gloria Londoño.
Description: [Wellington, FL] : Unbreakable Life Publishing, 2024. | Summary: A memoir of the author's kidnapping in her home country of Columbia, how she survived in captivity, and how she was able to heal from this experience and share it with others.
Identifiers: LCCN 2023923275 | ISBN 9798989603336 (pbk.)
Subjects: LCSH: Londoño, Gloria, 1972 – Biography. | Londoño, Gloria, 1972 – Kidnapping, 1997. | Kidnapping victims – Colombia – Biography. | Resilience (Personality trait). | Colombia. | BISAC: BIOGRAPHY & AUTOBIOGRAPHY / Memoirs. | BIOGRAPHY & AUTOBIOGRAPHY / Survival. | BIOGRAPHY & AUTOBIOGRAPHY / Women.
Classification: LCC HV6604.C65 L66 2024 | DDC 364.15/861 L--dc23
LC record available at https://lccn.loc.gov/2023923275

The stories in this book reflect the author's recollection of events. Some names, locations, and identifying characteristics have been changed to protect the privacy of those depicted.

To my grandfather, Benjamin, who told me to write this book and tell the story in English before he died. Thank you Grandpa. Rest in peace, 2021.

TABLE OF CONTENTS

Introduction 1

Chapter 1: From Bedroom Bars to Trunk Terror 5

Chapter 2: It's a Good Night Because I'm Still Alive 17

Chapter 3: Unexpected Kindness 23

Chapter 4: A Family's Unthinkable Farewell 43

Chapter 5: A Kiss of Hope 49

Chapter 6: Dad Doesn't Believe Me 73

Chapter 7: Living in the U.S.A. 89

Chapter 8: The Spark 99

Chapter 9: Constant Motion 107

Chapter 10: Darkness Into Light, Trauma Into Forgiveness . . 113

Conclusion 123

Additional Resources 125

INTRODUCTION

My name is Gloria Londoño. At age 25, I was the victim of a kidnapping that completely changed my life. Since then, I've battled my trauma and helped other women recover from their own. The purpose of this book is to help you overcome your traumas and practice forgiveness, so you can find the internal peace that so many of us seek.

Forgiveness to our parents, closest family, and friends is sometimes the most healing because the dynamics of these important relationships can create such great anger, madness, and pain. We keep forgetting that they treat us how they were taught to treat others, and their own childhoods often include trauma and pain. How can we judge them if they don't know better? They did the best they could to be there for us. They are also here to teach us unconditional love, and to be there so our forgiveness can allow us to grow and move to the next level of life.

It took me more than 17 years to find that forgiveness for my family and to find the strength within myself to face my trauma and overcome it. It also took a lot of therapy, self-work, and dedication to myself to transform my trauma into a blessing that I could pay forward. While there is always more to learn and always more self-growth possible, I am in a more comfortable place with my family, and what used to drag me down no longer does. With the help of my experiences, my hope is that it won't take you the same amount of time to process your traumas and find your way to forgiveness.

I am a soul who likes to use my story to empower others to feel better. Also, I am a visionary entrepreneur who has made a significant impact in the world of business and beyond. With a passion for innovation and a commitment to making a difference, I am proud to be a role model for aspiring entrepreneurs and a catalyst for positive community change.

I was born in Medellin, Colombia. My parents moved with me to Canada when I was nine months old. Seven years later, my parents moved back to Colombia. I am the oldest child and married for the first time at age 19. I had my daughter at 21. Today, I am 51 and a grandmother.

My journey into entrepreneurship began at the young age of 30. I displayed an innate curiosity and an unwavering drive for excellence from my early years. After my release from my kidnapping, my entrepreneurial spirit flourished.

I wasted no time diving into the world of business. I founded my first company, The Fresh Connection, a quality control inspection company for produce. Years later, I launched A&B Tropical Produce, which is still up and running today.

My dedication to innovation and ability to assemble a talented team quickly propelled the company to success.

After about five years, I changed careers and became a professional podcaster on a bilingual show that discusses depression, anxiety, and post-traumatic stress disorder (PTSD). I also saw the need to help other entrepreneurs fulfill their dreams. As a mentor coach, I help a lot of people create their companies for success.

This book is dedicated to my family and, in particular, to my parents. Through all my ordeals, including my kidnapping in Colombia, they also went through a lot of pain. I couldn't understand the decisions they made when I was kidnapped, and I harbored anger toward them for many years. Even after my release, I couldn't overcome that anger. And as a result, I was held hostage by myself—my mind and my memories.

One day, after a lot of personal growth, I realized I needed for my own sense of internal peace to understand the "why" behind my parents' actions. I put myself in their shoes, recreating the moments of my kidnapping but from their perspective! It was only then that I realized how much pain and suffering they must have felt, along with their desperation when they didn't have enough money to pay the ransom for my freedom. They couldn't help me, their daughter, and they must have felt so helpless and afraid for my life. They also sent my brothers away because they thought my brothers were in danger, too. They weren't just separated from me at that time, but all of their kids.

I hadn't been able to imagine everything that happened to my parents after I was kidnapped. Once I could, I began to empathize with them and understand their behavior. They did the best they could at that moment.

Writing this introduction, I've had to face how selfish I've been all these years, thinking they never loved me. The truth is that my parents love me so much I am able to be here, writing this book. I thank them for teaching me the best lesson of my life.

FROM BEDROOM BARS
TO TRUNK TERROR

When I was 16 years old, I planned to run away from home.

I always felt like my parents treated me differently from my brothers, and I had had enough. It was summer, and I was all packed and ready to go, but my parents found out. As punishment, they locked me in my bedroom for a month.

At the time, I thought it was the worst confinement I would experience, being sentenced to prison in my own room by my parents. Little did I know that this was only a precursor to a life-changing experience, one that would transform me completely. But at the time, I hated my parents. I could not understand why they locked me up instead of asking me to explain my reasons or exploring the root cause of why I wanted to escape. I never did drugs or drank alcohol. I wasn't even rebellious. I was just miserable watching all the fights and witnessing their constant mutual disrespect.

Nine years later, on October 22, 1997, I was 25 years old and heading home from university. I was in my third year, studying business administration at a university in Medellin, Colombia.

It had been a strange day. My boyfriend at the time had just told me that he was moving to the United States. I was jealous and really wanted to go with him. I rushed out of my economics class, my last class of the day, and hurriedly said goodbye to my friends. I wanted to get over to my boyfriend's place to help him pack, say farewell, and see if maybe he'd take me with him.

I raced out the burgundy-colored university door and ran down a narrow, paved walking path past other university students waiting to go into the classroom.

Nearby, a large outdoor market had juices and snacks for sale, which wasn't uncommon in Colombia. I saw another student I really liked at the market. He called after me, but I just waved and said, "Bye, bye." I couldn't stop to talk to him.

I ran down the university steps, the heels of my shoes clicking on the stone. I got into my car and drove around the parking lot to get to the exit. By the time I was 14 or 15, my dad was making good money. I was very flashy with new clothes all the time and a fancy car that I slowly drove when entering to the college parking so everyone could see me. I could feel their gaze. It made me feel happy to be noticed by so many people.

As I drove off, thinking about my boyfriend, the car in front of me suddenly stopped. I had to slam my foot on the brakes and screech to a halt so I wouldn't hit it. The other car just sat there. I couldn't drive around it or get back on the road.

Confused, I looked at my side mirrors to see what was going on. What I saw chilled me to the bone: A gun was pointed at my forehead.

"Get out, get out," said the man holding the gun.

I was frozen. I didn't know what to do. I couldn't think. I couldn't move. It felt like hours passed as I stared down its barrel.

"Get out of the car!" the man shouted.

I heard my father's voice in my head, *If someone tries to take your car, get out of the f***king car, and get down. Give it to them, and don't endanger your life.*

The guy with the gun grew impatient. With a growl, he released the gun's safety mechanism and pulled open my car door. He grabbed me by the back of the neck and ripped me out of the car, pressing the gun into my hair.

Ahead of me, there was a car up the street. Behind me was a bus full of people. I looked around wildly, wondering if anyone would do anything. Lots of people in Colombia carry guns. Someone on the street pulled out a gun and tried to save me.

I was so relieved—I could have kissed him! He didn't get very far, however, because the man holding me was just one of seven heavily armed, masked men standing around my car.

They all pointed guns at my would-be savior. "Do you want to die too, motherfucker?" they shouted at him.

My attackers picked me up and put me in the trunk of a car, then slammed the lid closed. Panicked in the dark, I didn't know what to do. I kept telling myself that I was going to die, that they were going to kill me.

In a moment of clarity, I remembered that I had one of those old brick-sized phones. I could call someone and get some help. *What if they stopped the car and opened the trunk while I was on the phone? What if they heard me talking?* My heart raced, and my fingers froze. If I made a call, I'd probably get killed the moment the car stopped and they opened the trunk.

I couldn't let that happen. I had to survive. My three-year-old daughter was waiting for me at home.

The car sped through bumpy streets, tossing me around. My body was taut and tense. It felt like they drove me around for hours, but it was really only about 20 minutes or so. Alone in the dark trunk, with all the bumps and dips, my mind played tricks on me.

The car pulled to a stop, and I heard the sound of a metal garage door opening. I heard voices, too, and they sounded young. I could hear them unloading the car. As soon as the trunk popped open, I held out my phone.

"Here, take it. I didn't make any calls. I promise. I didn't use it," I blurted. One of the guys snatched it away.

"Don't do any stupid shit, or you'll get hit. Got it?" someone else said.

The man closest to me grabbed the back of my neck and roughly forced my head down, pushing me forward through a house. I still have pain in my neck to this day.

I saw six tennis shoes moving with me. Six shoes meant three people, plus the guy who held my neck. Four kidnappers.

I was in survival mode. I felt like I was full of adrenaline and could see every little detail and hear every tiny sound. I felt almost superhuman.

They threw me into a room. I still wore my boots, and the first thing I started doing was walking loudly in the room so someone could hear me. I marched back and forth on the floor and sobbed. I knew I could be killed at any moment, but I didn't care.

After a few minutes, a man wearing a black face mask came into the room. The only thing I could see were his eyes. He handed me a piece of paper and a pen and told me to write down my name and my family information.

I thought my kidnappers were crazy and asked him if they were. How did they know I was the person they were after if they didn't even know who I was? Finally, he told me that if I didn't give them the information, it would be a long time before my family found out what happened to me.

I didn't have any choice. I had to do it! In tears, I wrote down the names of my family members, one by one, and their phone numbers.

As the man left the room, I said, "I hope I can get out soon, and I can see my little girl."

I cried and cried, feeling very afraid and wondering if I would ever see my family and daughter again. She would never understand what happened to her mommy.

I turned on the room light and sat on a bed. The room had a bathroom with a toilet but no toilet paper, and a shower that didn't work. Three more masked men entered. I tried to figure out who was in charge, but it was difficult.

Kidnapping, as horrible as it sounds, is a business where each participant gets paid for their role. One of the guys was about 6'1", with a big belly and a stronger voice than the others. He sounded like a boss and intimidated me. I guessed he was in his late 50s.

One of the others was skinny and about 5'1", just like me. His energy was more anxious, and he appeared to be a teenager. The third one was about 5'8". His voice was very calm, and his energy was quiet, making me think he was in his late 30s or early 40s. He also could have been the boss.

"We know your family has money, and they can afford to pay for your release," one said.

"Why are you guys doing this to me?" I asked.

"Because we know you are the only daughter of the family, and your father will pay right away for daddy's little girl."

I shook my head and explained to them that they had the wrong girl. My family wasn't going to pay anything to get me back. They didn't believe me, telling me that I must be daddy's little girl, and he'd pay anything.

I know my parents love me, but at the time I didn't feel that way, and I thought I could persuade them. It was what my brain told me to do to survive.

My captors refused to believe me. As they left the room, one of the men turned back and unscrewed the lightbulb from its fixture in the ceiling.

"What are you doing? Why are you taking that light?" I asked.

He said, "We don't want you to get creative, take the light bulb out, and do something crazy, like hurt yourself or try to hurt one of us."

They closed the door and left me in complete darkness, alone with my thoughts.

The sun began to set, and darkness fell.

OH MY GOD, I thought to myself, full of terror. *What is this!?*

After another 30 minutes or so, one of the men came back in, replaced the bulb, and turned on the light.

Handing me some oversized clothes, he said, "Remove all your clothes and your jewels. Take off your watch and boots. Wear these sweatpants and this shirt."

"Why?" I asked.

"Do what I am asking, and stop questioning everything. Just listen and do it!" he snapped.

I had no choice but to just do it.

I removed my clothes in front of him, feeling very humiliated. I also worried what he might do once my clothes were off.

I was too hot in the sweatpants and begged my captors to give me scissors so I could cut a slit in the pants. But they refused, saying, "No, we can't give you scissors. You could hurt yourself or us."

Finally, I asked if I could give them my pants and let them cut the slits. One of the men agreed. I told him where to cut the pants, and he did. In that moment, I realized everything here might be able to be negotiated. Maybe I could use that to my advantage.

I fell asleep but kept waking up every two hours to pitch dark and quiet.

They gave me a blanket but didn't feed me that night. I don't recall if I was hungry, but I didn't care if I ate or not. The room was stuffy and smelled old. Many, many times, I asked, *Why me, why me, why me!?*

What did I do to deserve this? I'd been a good person, and yet I'd had hard moments. I almost lost my daughter when she was born prematurely and she couldn't breathe. Since I was so petite, they scheduled me for a C-section at 39 weeks so I didn't have to give birth naturally. I was ready to be done with the pregnancy at that point. I was huge and in pain all the time. But the doctor made a mistake. He thought I was at 39 weeks, but I was only at 38 weeks, when it is still dangerous.

When I went in for surgery, I wasn't anesthetized completely. I knew when they took my daughter out, but I was listening and listening, and I couldn't hear her cry. I knew something was wrong.

After several minutes, I heard her crying, but the doctors rushed her out of the room before I could hold her. My daughter was put in an incubator to keep her alive.

A doctor told me that she couldn't breathe, and I just kept thinking to myself, *Why me?*

In my country, there is a tradition that for 40 days after a mother gives birth, she gets to lay in bed and is treated like a princess. The baby is brought to her to nurse, and she is fed special meals. I didn't get to experience that. Instead, the day after I had major surgery, I was walking around worrying about my daughter.

Three days after she was born, I was in the waiting room when the doctor came to see me and told me that my daughter was dying. They brought me to sit with her. I reached into the incubator and held her hand. I talked to her and begged her not to leave. Somehow, she started to stabilize and came back to me.

Days later, she needed plasma, and my mom had to rush out of the hospital late at night to buy the plasma and bring it to her in order to save her life. She was so desperate, she pulled out on the wrong side of the road and drove against traffic the whole way, but she got the plasma that saved my baby girl.

When my daughter was 10 days old, the doctor came to me again and told me I needed to get a priest to perform the last rites over her. I was devastated. She'd fought so hard, and we'd done so much. But they were sure she was dying.

I sat with her and held her hand again while the priest performed his rites before the incubator. Again, I pleaded with her to come back to me.

She did—but she wasn't out of the woods yet. She got sicker and sicker due to a staph infection, and we moved her from the clinic into a hospital. We had no way of knowing if she'd make it through the night. The head nurse told me to bring a radio so they could put on different music every day and see if she reacted to the music, feeling alive again.

Day by day she was getting better with the upbeat background music—my miracle baby started getting stronger and healthier. That ordeal had impacted me so much.

After being kidnapped, I found myself again asking God if I would see her again and asking, *Why am I here?*

The second day, the kidnappers brought me breakfast. To my surprise, it was good—hot scrambled eggs with onions and tomatoes, toast, and coffee. I don't drink coffee, but that day it was amazing. I ate it quickly and couldn't help but be reminded of how my nanny used to serve me breakfast at home. I had been a spoiled brat when I didn't like the food. I had had it so good, and now things were so bad.

I felt the urge to go to the bathroom, but there was no toilet paper. I knocked on the door a couple times asking for some, and one of the men responded and told me I had to "deal with it." He reminded me that I wasn't staying in a hotel.

He also told me, "We've decided not to contact your family for fifteen days so they will become desperate. By the time we contact them, they will be really desperate and ready to pay for you," one of the men said.

"Wow!" I said. "That means I will be here with you for a long time."

"That depends on your family. We can move quickly or we can move slowly," he told me.

My hopes fell. It was late October, and I hoped I would be with my family by Christmas. It was going to be a long journey.

The kidnappers left.

I felt desolate. I knew some people who were kidnapped and didn't come back home again. But now that it was happening to me, I realized how vulnerable I was and how much empathy I felt for others who had experienced the same thing.

IT'S A GOOD NIGHT
BECAUSE I'M STILL ALIVE

A single day can feel like weeks in isolation.

Alone in a dark room, I wasn't sure how much time had passed. When I couldn't take it anymore, I knocked on the door a couple of times to ask.

"Listen, you can't continue knocking on the door all of the time," a male voice said. "This is the last time you do this because next time, I will slap you to get you to stop!"

"OK, I understand, but what time is it for the last time?" I asked.

"3:30 p.m.," he told me.

"What time will my dinner be?" I asked.

"Later," another man said curtly.

That later felt like a lot later to me. I said to myself, *Let's go to sleep and see if the time goes faster. I can get more news later,* and I fell into such a deep sleep that they had to wake me for dinner.

One of my captors put food on paper plates on the floor next to the door. It was rice, meat, and salad with pineapple juice. I ate the meal with gratitude because it really could have been a lot worse. I was surprised by how hungry I was, given the stressful situation. When I finished, the same man came in and picked up the plates then left.

I could brush my teeth, but I couldn't rinse my mouth because I didn't have water. I tried to sleep some more. My mind and body were being pushed to the extreme, and my energy was low.

I woke in the middle of the night, and it was pitch dark. *Why me? GOD! WHY ME!* I cried like a little girl.

I slept a lot during the day, so the night felt much longer. I talked to my God about every single detail of my life, reviewing everything and promising Him the things I would do if I could go home and see my daughter again. It was weird! I never felt I was going to die, but I relived my life for hours.

On the third morning, my captors opened the door. This time, they brought the same breakfast but gave it to me in my bed like room service.

"Thank you," I said.

"Today, you can take a shower," one of the men told me.

I was so happy! I smelled terrible after two days with no way to clean myself and stuck in a hot room. Not to mention my bathroom situation.

I asked when.

"After your breakfast, I'll come back and take you out of the room to the bathroom to have the shower," my kidnapper explained.

Good. Now I would see where I was.

"Don't knock on the door again just because you get impatient," he went on. "This is not about your time. It's about when we want to do stuff. Feel lucky that we are giving you food and taking you for a shower. In other cases, people don't have that option."

"Why do you think I am getting special treatment?" I asked.

"Because the order from the top is that we can't touch you or treat you badly anymore. You are protected," he said.

"Order from whom!?" I asked.

"Stop with your questions! Isn't it enough that I'm coming back for you to take your shower?"

I couldn't believe what he just said. I would still be a captive, but at least they wouldn't treat me badly.

I finished my breakfast. I took my time because if I ate it too quickly, my wait for the shower would feel a lot longer. Finally, the man came back.

"Turn around so that I can cover your eyes and take you out," he said.

He said he was going to hold me and walk me to the bathroom. He explained that when we were in the bathroom, he would let me remove my clothes so I could shower.

He started walking, and I felt a bright light on my skin. It was a weird sensation. I was surprised how my body could pick up on the new light, even with my eyes covered.

It was a nice sensation, like a dream, and I wondered where I was and how this place looked. As much as I wanted to rip the cover off my eyes, I knew I needed to behave or they might not let me shower again. We went into what I guessed was a bathroom.

"You can remove the cover from your eyes and start undressing," the man said.

"But you're still here. How am I going to undress in front of you?!" I asked nervously.

"Do you want to take a shower or not?" he replied.

"I want to take a shower," I said. Who cared if he watched me? I also remembered they weren't allowed to touch or hurt me, so I started undressing. I felt humiliated but I needed to wash off. I smelled rank.

I turned on the left knob for hot water, and my captor laughed.

"You're so spoiled! There's no hot water for you there. You need to take a cold-water shower," he said, laughing at me again. "And you can't make any noise."

When my body hit the cold water, I wanted to scream. But soon my body got used to the cold water, and my pleasure returned at getting clean. When I found soap, it was like I found a treasure, even if it appeared to have a pubic hair on it.

I realized, nope, I can't say anything. I removed the hair and flicked it into the water. I didn't know the next time I would get to take another shower, so I enjoyed every minute.

The man said I had five minutes to finish. He stood outside the shower stall, unable to see me while I was taking a shower. I was lucky to have some privacy and felt some relief from all that had been going on in my mind.

When I showered at home, I focused on cleaning myself with the best or most expensive beauty brands. This time, I didn't worry about that. I was happy to just feel clean and energized!

I wrapped myself in a towel, and the man let me get dressed in private. I detangled my hair with my fingers as best I could.

A lot of it was dropping out and getting stuck around my fingers. It was the stress. I decided to save the hairs so I would have something to do in the darkness.

There were no phones, television, magazines, or books. There wasn't even any art to look at on the walls.

I thought I was going crazy, counting the tiles on the floor, counting the panes of glass in the window and trying to guess if my head could fit through it. When my hair started falling out, counting the hairs was just another way to keep my sanity.

I fell asleep back in my darkened room. When I woke up, it was time for dinner. They had prepared arepas made of stuffed cornmeal. They also brought me tuna and pineapple juice, and I ate with no problem.

When a kidnapper came in to take my plate and paper cup, he said, "Goodnight."

"Goodnight," I replied. I figured it was a good night because I was still alive.

UNEXPECTED KINDNESS

O n the 11th day of my captivity, I woke up and felt like I didn't need to cry anymore. I was getting sick, and my energy was very low. I didn't even want to live because I was so exhausted.

When breakfast arrived, my captor told me to get up.

"I can't," I said. "I don't have the energy."

He put the breakfast down. "What do you feel?" he asked.

"I have a huge pain in the back of my right side, and I can't feel my body very well," I said.

He grabbed me and pulled me up, trying to get me to stand. My body didn't want to respond. He tried to grab me again, and again I went down.

"Oh, you're depressed," he said in a soft voice. "I am going to sit down with you and hold you, and I will give you some food so you get vital energy."

It was exactly what I needed to feel better. There was a transfer of energy between us from his kindness and willingness to help me. It was something that changed my view about him.

I was numb and didn't want to talk too much.

"I need to come in more often because I will not let you die," he said. "It isn't good for you or us."

"Because you can't get your money, right?" I asked.

He didn't say anything. He just made a grunting sound with his mouth and kept feeding me.

"Go to sleep and rest," he said when I finished. "I'll come back later to see how you are doing."

His kindness overwhelmed me. I didn't think I could feel grateful to one of my captors, but in that moment, I really did. Later, I learned that it is common among kidnap victims.

"Thank you so much for being with me and for making sure I am OK," I said.

After this depression episode my thinking got clear and came to the realization that I needed to accept the situation the way it was and enjoy every minute being alive. Then my mind went into "fight or flight" mode and I started to use survival mode and thinking on a strategy to keep calm to survive each moment.

I don't know how long I was asleep, but when I woke up, he was sitting on the end of the bed with a large gun.

"What are you doing here?" I asked.

"Nothing, I just came here to be with you so you'd feel better," he said.

"Why do you have that firearm?"

"I need to have it with me at all times," he said. I didn't believe him. "Sit here with me, let's talk."

"About what?" I asked.

"About anything."

"Why are you are doing what you are doing?"

"Like what?" he asked.

"Why you are in the kidnapping business?"

"Well, it is what it is," he said with a shrug.

"Do you think there are better ways to make money other than this?" I asked.

"The opportunities are not the same."

"What about family? Do you have any?" I asked.

"We can't talk about that," he said. "Why don't you tell me about your family. What you said the day we kidnapped you stuck in my mind."

"Well, it is a long story," I said. "My father treats my mother and me very badly."

For as long as I could remember, my father had been mentally and verbally abusive to us. He showed preference to my two brothers. Even though I knew deep inside my father loved me and wanted to protect me, the way he showed it was so cruel, it was often hard to believe.

My father never believed anything I said was true. He laughed at my dreams and told me I couldn't do anything in life. Because I was divorced and had a daughter, he supported me but wanted to continue to control all aspects of my life. I lived in a cage with a golden chain.

My captor couldn't believe what he was hearing.

"It's time for me to go. I shouldn't be here with you. I am risking my life and the operation just being here," he said, starting to rise.

"Don't go. Stay another minute with me, please," I practically begged.

"No, I can't. If I can, I'll try to come in again later but I can't promise anything," he said and left.

If I could get this man to be my friend, things could change. I felt determined to survive and get out of this place, no matter what it took.

On day 15, I heard the sounds of a helicopter. It was close, and it seemed to be hovering above where we were.

Wump. Wump. Wump.

The sound of the rotating blades got louder until I could feel the vibrations through my entire body.

"What is going on here!?" I said aloud, wishing I had a window. Sometimes, talking to myself was the only voice I heard for hours at a time.

I wondered if a helicopter meant that law enforcement found us and was coming to rescue me. It gave me a glimmer of hope that soon this nightmare would be over.

Immediately, one of my kidnappers came into the room with a huge gun and a grenade on his waist. He seemed very anxious.

"Listen, motherfucker, if they come for you, we are all going to die together. I don't give a shit, and I'll blow this building and all of us up together," he said.

I went straight into a panic mode. My body shook. I was so distraught that I don't know how I managed to crawl under the space beneath my little bed, between the floor and the mattress. It was a combination of anxiety and panic attack.

Please, please don't let them come for me, I prayed. *Please, please make the helicopter go away.* I didn't want to die like that!

I heard all the kidnappers "shushing" each other. The place fell silent.

"Be quiet, stop crying!" the guy with the grenade hissed at me. He left and slammed the door closed.

They didn't bring me dinner, which was weird, and everything was quiet. Maybe I was alone.

I started knocking on the door very lightly to see if anyone could hear me. I did that three times, and no one answered. I thought it could be my opportunity to escape, but minutes later, I heard the garage door open and a car pull in.

Footsteps approached my room, and the man who had been nice to me opened the door.

He told me we were leaving. At first, I got really excited, thinking I was finally going home. He sneered at me and grabbed me by my neck.

"You wish. I'm going to put you inside the trunk of the car again, and we're going to move you to another location. This place is hot now."

That meant the police group, called GAULA (*Los Grupos of Acción Unificada por La Libertad Personal* or Unified Action Groups for Personal Freedom), in charge of finding and recovering missing and kidnapped people was nearby. I was scared but also curious about changing locations. I hoped the new place was bigger and had better light with a full bathroom.

I realized I might not be freed anytime soon.

I just wanted my situation to get a little more comfortable, so I could survive the ordeal.

They put me in the trunk again, but this time was different. I felt the movement of the car, the smell of gasoline, and the sounds of other cars and motorcycles. It was fun to hear the everyday sounds of life again, and the ride distracted me from any nervousness I might have felt.

The car stopped, and the kidnappers opened what sounded like another garage. Someone knocked on the trunk.

"Are you ok?" a familiar voice asked. It was the man I knew best.

"Yes," I said.

"I am going to open the trunk now, you know the deal," he said.

I told him I did. He opened the trunk, and this time, he grabbed me more gently by my neck.

"We're going in now," he said.

My new room was bigger with a little window, and I could see the light coming in. There was even a full bathroom. I had grown to feel a great deal of humility and appreciation for every little thing I received. I felt myself transforming.

If I could be humble and grateful in this situation, things would be better or even change. If they killed me, at least I did what I was supposed to be doing in life. I began saying thank you for everything—my food, water, and shower. I noticed my kidnappers' attitudes were changing dramatically, too.

They started acting nicer toward me. The youngest man brought me breakfast and stayed in the room to talk to me. They remained masked, and I never saw his face or the faces of the others.

I heard some salsa music, and he asked, "Do you like this song?"

"Yes, I like it! It is very cool," I said.

He replied, "Do you want to dance with me?"

"Why not!?"

We began salsa dancing, and for a second, I forgot where I was, even though my dance partner's face was concealed.

I could differentiate between my captors with their voices and body types, even the way they smelled. The young man said it was great dancing with me.

"Me too, thank you!" I said excitedly.

"We can do it another time if you want."

"OK, cool," I said. He left and came back again a little while later.

"I love to dance with you," he said and closed the door.

Uh-oh, this guy is acting weird! It could be dangerous. The young man usually came in the morning. The soft-spoken man who comforted me when I was depressed, and to whom I was growing attached, came in the afternoons.

My room was always dark, and when they entered, they left the door open. It teased me. I thought more than once about escaping but I was scared, not knowing what would be on the other side.

Two of the men began to wear cologne, and it seemed like they wanted to impress me. I kept quiet about it, but I took note of everything that was going on.

I lost track of the time. Hours, days, weeks all blended into one, and I lived the same reel of time over and over. But I began to sense that the young man who brought me breakfast was starting to develop real feelings for me.

"I need to talk to you," he said after bringing me breakfast.

My heart started to pound, and I was getting nervous, especially when he checked the door two times as if he was making sure no one was there. As a captive, my senses worked like never before. Everything was amplified.

The guy closed the door completely, and I asked, "What is wrong?" I spoke with a strong voice because I knew he was doing something wrong, something he was not supposed to do.

"I want to tell you something about me," he said. "I do not know why I have these feelings for you, but I am in love with you!"

"What!? I don't understand what you're saying!" I cried.

"You know exactly what I am talking about," he said. Then he added, "I know you feel the same for me."

"What?" I said. "I think you are confused about what you are telling me. I don't have feelings for you or anyone here. How could I have feelings like that, especially in the situation I am in?"

"I do not care if you do not love me," the kidnapper responded.

I was so confused. I worried about the situation and felt I was in danger if I was to say no to him. He might abuse me, or worse.

"I want to show my love to you," he said.

My eyes popped wide open, and I grew nervous.

"This is the way I am going to show you my love," he said, and he started removing his face cover.

"No, please! I do not want to see your face, please don't! I do not want to recognize you for the rest of my life! Please, no!" I cried.

He removed his mask anyway, and I turned my face to the side.

"Look at me!" he demanded.

"NO!" I shouted.

He told me to look again, and I still refused. If any of the men thought I could recognize them, I didn't think they'd keep me alive. I was getting annoyed with him.

Finally, I asked, "Are you sure you want me to see your face?"

"Yes," he insisted.

"OK, fine, I will!" I snapped.

I was freaking out inside, but I had asked him three times if he was sure. He was the one risking everything. If his boss found out he broke the rules, he'd be a liability to them, and I didn't think they'd think twice about punishing him. If he was going to keep saying yes, I didn't care.

"I love you, and this is the way to show my love to you," he said.

When I turned around, it was a major surprise. He was so young, even younger than me, and far younger than I expected. I was 25 years old, and he was probably 16 or 17.

"Why are you doing this!? You're so young! Why don't you go to school and do something better for yourself?" I asked. I was terrified for both of us.

He told me that there weren't many opportunities for him, and his family needed the money.

"Wow! Does your mother know about this?" I asked.

"Not really," he said.

Then he heard a noise, and he put his face cover back on quickly.

"Please don't say anything to anyone about what I did," he said.

He left the room, and my intuition told me I needed to tell someone. If they found out what he did, I'd be in trouble, too.

The next day, two of the men, the boss and the tall guy with the big belly—the man I had grown fond of—came into my room. They said they needed to talk to me.

The big guy said, "We finally want to start communicating with your family, and we need you to write a letter so they can see you are still alive."

"Oh, finally. So, that way I can go home in December," I said.

"You wish," he said sarcastically. "We'll bring you the newspaper tomorrow, so you can write down that you're still alive and give them the date."

All I could say was, "OK." They left.

I was so excited because it meant I was probably going home soon! That night, the soft-spoken man came in and asked about my day. I wondered if I should tell him about the young man.

"My day was good, thank you. What about yours?" I tried to make conversation.

"It was OK."

"You're so lucky that you can be out and about, and I am in this situation," I said.

He closed his eyes and took a deep breath and said, "You will be out, too, soon."

"When!?" I asked.

"That depends on your family and how quickly they will pay. There's still a lot of processes to go through, so this will take a long time. And if your family doesn't pay, we will need to sell you to another organization that operates from the mountains," he explained.

"Oh no, please help me. If I go to the mountains, what will happen to me?" I asked.

"You will walk for days and sleep at night, and you will need to do everything outside. They don't care if they take one or two or three years to release you because you are cheaper to maintain," he said.

"You know I have a daughter who is three years old," I said.

"Yes, I know. I studied you for three months before we kidnapped you," he said. "I know how you dress, where you go shopping, what kind of car you drive, and the way you drive. I know your boyfriend, your friends, your class routine, everything. Why do you think we needed to use two cars to stop you and kidnap you!?"

I said, "Why?"

"Because you drive extremely fast, and if you saw we were following, we would not have been available to catch you."

This was a surprise to me. He was giving me a lot of information, and something was telling me to start testing the waters with him about what happened with the younger man two days earlier.

"So many people are here," I said.

"There are six people," he said.

"Is it always the same?" I asked.

He said, "No, we take turns going out because this is like a job. When it is your day off, you can leave."

"Are you bringing me my food tomorrow?" I asked.

"Yes, in the afternoon," he said. "Why are you asking?"

Now that we were having a conversation, I wanted to see if I could trust him and somehow use that to my advantage. We talked for a little bit until I was sure that he would keep a secret for me. I just needed someone to talk to. I needed to feel like someone heard me.

"When you come back tomorrow, I need to tell you something

personal," I told him.

"What? Now I am curious," he said with a nice tone. There was nothing to worry about. I knew he had feelings for me, and I had feelings for him. It was a case of Stockholm Syndrome, a coping mechanism that occurs when hostages develop a psychological bond with their captors.

I was in a very vulnerable place, where any little nice thing became important, and I was getting attached to the only person who showed me compassion—and whom I needed to survive. It can easily be confused with love, as I experienced with the younger man.

"You're not going to tell me?" he asked. I got the sense he expected me to say that I liked him. "OK, if you're not going to tell me, I will be thinking about you all night."

He grabbed my leg, and I didn't care. I even kind of liked it. I knew by then I could take advantage of the situation.

He left and I went to sleep. Each day, it was getting easier to fall asleep. I got into the mindset that I would see my daughter and could stop feeling nervous about my future. Deep inside, I believed that everything was going to be OK.

The next day, the young guy brought me breakfast, and I saw that his energy had changed. I wondered if he thought that he had made a huge mistake.

"Thank you for my breakfast," I said.

"You're welcome," he said in a very strange tone.

I started to get anxious. My body was telling me something was wrong.

Four hours later, three men showed up in my room, and I got super worried. It was the soft-spoken man, the boss, and another man whom I had never seen before.

"You know we told you we wanted you to write a letter for your family, and today is the day," one of the men said. "We brought the newspaper so when you write it, they will have a reference that you are still alive because you wrote down today's news headlines."

"Ok, what do you want me to write?" I asked.

"Anything you want. Tell your family that you are OK and that you can't wait to be back home and that you're in a complicated situation," he said. "Tell them you are afraid that you will be killed, you want to see your daughter again, and you need them to pay the ransom as quickly as possible, and then write down these headlines from today's newspaper."

He handed me a pen and paper, and I started writing.

When I finished, one man read the letter over and said it was fine. One of the younger men left with the letter I wrote, but the boss and my soft-spoken man, whom I started calling Henry in my head, stayed behind.

All I wanted was to go home and be with my daughter again. In the letter, I wrote how much I was suffering and how I couldn't take it anymore. I hoped that my words would communicate my pain.

To me, writing the letter felt desperate but also hopeful. It might accelerate the process for my kidnappers getting paid and my release.

"I need to talk to you in private," I said to the boss. "I need you to promise me that if I tell you something, I will not have to suffer any consequences."

"That depends," he said, crossing his arms. I felt confident I was doing the right thing.

"The guy who brings me the breakfast, you know who he is," I began.

"Yes, of course, the young guy," he said.

"Yes. Three days ago, he took off his mask and revealed his face to me. He told me he did it because he loves me. I insisted that he not do it, and he insisted that it was the way for him to show me his love for me."

His eyes grew large.

"Wait! You just said that this guy revealed his face to you?"

"Yes!"

"Oh boy, oh boy. What has this little fucker done? We'll talk later," he said. He closed the door hard and left rapidly.

I fell to my knees, and I couldn't stop shaking. I felt terrible until I reminded myself that I did what I needed to do.

That same day, the young guy came to my room with lunch. His energy had changed for the better, and he was nice to me.

I could tell they hadn't told him anything about what I said earlier, and I felt like a traitor, even though he was my kidnapper. That was the last time I ever saw him. No one told me what happened to him.

One day, the boss entered my room.

"Hello Gloria, how are you feeling today?"

That was a surprise for me to hear, especially when he called me by name. He was being extra nice.

"I am fine, thank you. I want to go home soon."

"I don't know about that," he said. "But one thing I want to say to you today is I am very surprised, and I admire you big time."

"Why?" I asked.

"Because you risked your life to tell the truth," he said. "You could have saved that information and waited until we released you. But you recognized this guy will hurt us and the entire operation.

Because of that, I am coming to say thank you."

"I appreciate you telling me that, but what am I getting from this? Just the thank you?"

I had a good head for business. My kidnappers wanted to get paid. As strange as it sounded, I was their best chance at making that happen, and that put me in a more powerful position than I realized before.

"I will promise to save your life if you can help us make your family pay the ransom money," he said.

"Well, that's a tricky deal because you'll secure my life if my family pays, not because I told you the truth," I said.

"Well, I need your family to pay."

"That is not in my control. I told the truth to save my life, and I hope you can honor that, even if my family doesn't pay," I said. "I told you at the start that my family doesn't care that much for me."

"Wow! You really are negotiating for your life," he said.

"Well, it's the only real thing I have, other than this pair of shorts and this T-shirt. I want to see and raise my daughter, so I would like you to think hard on this," I said.

"You know what, Gloria? Let me hug you," he said. "You deserve to live and see your daughter again, and I hope your family pays."

I didn't feel as scared as I was with the young man. This man somehow made me feel safer and more comfortable. He was kind, and I could tell that he had respect for me.

There's a moment when a woman knows she "has" a man wrapped around her finger. I was starting to feel that way with him.

"I want that, too, but it's not in my hands, remember that!" I said.

"I have so much admiration for you, for what you did. I honor you for being a very strong little woman," he said and then left.

I couldn't believe it. I tell my daughter all the time that it doesn't matter what situation you are in, always tell the truth and just the truth. I know from firsthand experience it might save your life.

The kidnappers told me that next we were going to talk to my family because they had asked for proof that I was alive.

"Everything depends on what they do after they believe you're alive," the boss said, "I cannot give you more information."

Then he left the room. I was going to talk to my family for the first time since being taken. I was so anxious that I couldn't sleep that night.

I wanted my parents to know I was alive because I wanted them to help get me out. But a part of me worried about what they would say.

A FAMILY'S
UNTHINKABLE
FAREWELL

Before being kidnapped, I'd never had an experience that forced me to truly slow down and experience humility and gratitude. Life had always been about going and going and going.

Through my ordeal, I felt like I was becoming someone different, a better version of myself.

The mental image of my release helped me to stay optimistic, even in the most desperate and desolate times. I expected to see a lot of people waiting for me with flowers, and everybody would be happy. I imagined people would come to my house and gather around me and be happy for my freedom and restarting my life. I anticipated how happy I'd be with my daughter.

I tried to maintain those thoughts. But on the day of the call, I was mentally and emotionally exhausted. A knock on the door for breakfast woke me up. I was going to talk to my family for the first time after two months in captivity.

"Gloria, we're going to have the call when we're in the city in one hour," said one of my captors as he took away my plate.

"For real? Oh my God, I'm so freaking happy, I can't wait!" I said. I felt a kind of happy anxiety. "I'm so nervous now. If my family agrees to pay, I'm going to be free."

Maybe an hour later, three men came in with a radio antenna.

"Why are you guys bringing a radio instead of a cell phone?" I asked.

"Because it's harder for them to track us. If we use a cell phone, it will be very easy for them."

My hands shook, but I was ready.

"Hello, hello, hello," they said, testing the signal.

Finally, they found the signal and gave my family the correct frequency.

When I heard my father's voice, I trembled, and my heart beat so loudly I wondered if my father could hear it.

"I love you," he said.

"How are you, Father?" I asked.

"Are you OK?"

"I just want to go home," I said.

"Yes, I know you want to go home, but I have some bad news for you. We don't have money to pay for this kidnapping. And I cannot do anything else," he said. "All I can say to you is whatever God has planned with those guys is what he wants to happen."

Instead of getting to go home, I was stuck. I sank into a deep, deep sadness. I couldn't believe what he was saying! I could not even comprehend it.

I shook my head over and over.

"I can't stay here," I said. "It can't be true."

"Don't worry. You're in God hands," my father said. "God bless you. I'm going to put you on with your mother so you can hear her voice, and she will hear you for the last time."

When he said that, I almost collapsed. Hear my mother's voice for the last time? I didn't want to hear any more.

"No more, I can't take this anymore," I said.

One of the kidnappers must have seen my face grow pale. He held out his arms and held me because I might faint.

My mother said the same things as my father, but I also heard her breaking down.

"You heard your father," she said. "The only thing I can say is your daughter is going to be in good hands. I love you and God bless you."

When she said that, my captors looked at each other as if they were thinking, *What the heck happened here? What is this?*

It took me years and years to understand why my parents did that. I wanted only for my story and my emotions to be validated. To feel abandoned by your family in a situation like that, not knowing what was going on with them, was terrible. It was a lot for me to process—one trauma on top of another.

I had no idea what was coming next! There were men I was going to be sold to who might kill me. They weren't going to give a shit about me after they heard what my family said.

I was sad, but I went into survival mode and tried bribing my captors. I offered to give them my car and apartment. I begged them to accept my offer. Anything so I could go home.

They left me alone after the call with my parents, and it felt like a long, long time before Henry brought me a very late lunch.

"I can't believe what I heard this morning," he said.

It felt good to talk to him. He was getting attached to me, too, like reverse Stockholm Syndrome.

He left me to eat, but I was stressed and in disbelief and had no appetite. My body balked at every bite I forced down.

I knew I had to eat because I didn't know when I'd eat again, and I needed to stay strong. I didn't have the luxury of saying, "I don't want to eat right now. I can eat at my next meal."

I ate slowly, still shocked about what had happened with my family. I assumed that my family had been worrying about me, desperate and searching. But my dad had been cold and distant.

That had been devastating. It was like they didn't miss or worry about me. I thought they'd tell me they were doing whatever they could to get me back.

A KISS OF HOPE

"What is going to happen to me?" I asked the next morning when one of the men brought me breakfast.

"I'm not allowed to talk about that. Just eat your breakfast," he told me firmly.

I ate, but I was still exhausted and in a daze. Everything felt surreal. Was this happening? Had my family really abandoned me?

With nothing else for me to do, my imagination went wild. I was anxious, crying, and my mind wouldn't stop.

The same man came in to get my plate and asked if I wanted to shower.

At that moment, I felt like a shower would be the cure for everything I felt. The room was hot, and I felt sweaty. Even though the shower blasted ice cold water, it was refreshing and helped to calm my wild mind.

I put my head in the cold water, and all the heat released from my body. I could practically feel steam coming off my scalp. It was a moment of disconnect from the situation, like a reset button.

I told myself I was going to survive. I was going to get out of there, see my daughter and hug her again. The cold water made me feel alive again, so I knew I had to keep going.

One of the other good things about the shower was that I had a little privacy. My kidnappers usually stood in the room with me when I changed but never looked at me. They didn't peek in the small shower or try to get in with me. I never felt like they wanted to rape me or shame me.

That privacy meant a lot to me, especially since it gave me space to think about things. I felt newly determined to get out of this and see my daughter again. I wasn't giving up, and I wasn't down for the count.

Now, my mind could start working on a plan. Henry.

I saw that Henry had been nicer with me than the other men, even when I was first kidnapped. Maybe I needed to use my "woman power" to attract him so he would protect me and keep me safe. It was the only way I thought I could get back to my life.

I saw Henry as a way to freedom, like I had when I was 19. I married then to get away from my father and have my own life. It was a way out. Henry could be another way out.

I had nothing left to lose. I could use my seductive charms to get him to help me. I knew deep down that if he became emotionally attached, he would do anything for me.

That day, Henry brought me lunch and was especially nice. I think he felt sorry for me because of my family.

He sat down next to me.

"Are you going to stay?" I asked.

"Yeah. I want to enjoy your lunch with you and chat," he said.

I couldn't see his face behind the mask, but I could see his eyes, and I could tell he felt something for me.

"I'm happy you're here. I really, really need it," I said, trying out my charms on him. I ate slowly.

Henry had a lot of sympathy for me, and I felt like something was going to happen.

I was right. One day, when I was in a really dark, depressed place, he took me in his arms. I felt like he transferred energy to me, like a phone low on battery bursting back to life once it's plugged in.

I didn't want to leave his arms or his hug. I wanted to stay there. We had a connection.

He left soon after our embrace but started coming more often to check on me.

I liked him a lot and preferred his company to the other men. I was afraid to ask questions about who was coming to bring my food because I didn't want them to know that I had a connection with Henry or that I was interested in him.

Little by little, I asked, "So, you're the guy from breakfast."

"Yes."

"Oh, so the other guy will bring me dinner, right?"

"No, no, the other guy who works at night will bring it to you."

When it was finally Henry's turn to bring me food, I was so happy.

"Are you going to stay here the day and bring me dinner?" I asked.

"Yes, because I'm covering for the other guy, so I'm going to bring you dinner and be here all day."

It was the perfect opportunity to see what power I had over him. But I didn't say anything.

He brought lunch and left it.

"Can you come later, and we can sit and talk?" I asked when he returned.

When Henry came in later, I asked him why he was doing this and if he had a family. He didn't give a lot of details, but he did say he had a family. I didn't know if he had kids.

I put my head on his shoulder, and he hugged me. At first, I thought it was just sympathy.

I said, "You smell good."

"Thank you," he said. "It's the soap."

Of course, something as simple as nice soap was like high-end cologne for me in this situation.

"Are you taking care of me tonight?" I asked.

"Why?"

"I don't know why. Because I like when you come and visit with me, so we can talk and I can feel better," I said.

"What we going to talk about?" he asked.

"Anything, nothing in particular," I said.

"Let me see what happens," he replied. "I'll let you know. If I stay, I'll come for a short visit."

"OK!" I said excitedly.

"You should eat a little faster because the food isn't really warm like you like it," Henry said.

He'd gotten to know some personal things about me just from watching me and he remembered my preferences. For him to care like that, he was a lot more interested in me than anyone else in that group. That little detail meant a lot.

He made a sound, and I looked into his eyes–the only part I could see of him.

He said, "I'm sorry, it must have been devastating for you, with your family."

"Yeah. I didn't really expect it," I said. Tears wet my cheeks.

"No, don't cry."

"I don't have any other options here," I said, shaking my head. I needed him to feel bad for me and to want to help me.

"You mentioned the option of your car and apartment," reminding me of what I'd said when I was panicked.

"I don't know if you're going to accept it," I said.

"Well, we're thinking about it because we don't know what else to do after we heard you on the call with your family," Henry said.

"It would be really great if you accept it," I said, still trying to persuade him.

"Do you know what happens if you don't pay or your family doesn't pay?" he asked.

I'd asked one of the other guys that question. Henry might be able to confirm what the other man had told me about being sold.

"What?" I asked nervously. "Is it true that if my family doesn't pay, they will sell me to people in the mountains?"

His respond was, "Yes, we'll sell you."

"Sell me to whom?" I asked, panic rising in my chest.

"To other groups," he said. I already knew that, but I wanted to confirm with him.

"Where will I go, and how long will I be there?" I asked.

"Two things: One, if this happens, you'll live in the mountains with them, but you won't be in one place. You'll walk through the mountains because they're nomads. They don't want to get found," he said. "The second thing, and the worst part, is they can sell you whenever they want or keep you. It can be a year, four years, or they'll never let you go."

My eyes opened wide, like they were going to pop out of my head.

The only good thing about that was I'd be out of this room, and I'd be outside in nature. Everything else just sounded awful. I couldn't be without my daughter.

"No, no, no. Please, don't let that happen," I cried. "I can't be away from my daughter that long."

Henry was on my left side. I grabbed his arm and begged him not to sell me to them.

"I will do anything, *anything*. Don't sell me like that," I pleaded.

He had a huge firearm in his lap, but he put his arms around me in a tight hug.

He could be my savior.

"Don't worry," he said. "I'm going to try my best to help you."

I felt a little hope in my heart.

"Thank you. Thank you so much," I said.

As he lifted my tray to go, he said, "I'll bring you dinner later."

It was a few days later when the boss showed up with Henry.

"Write a letter to your family saying that you want them to give us the cost of your apartment and the car," he said. "We'll send it to your friend."

After my parents said they couldn't pay, I told my kidnappers I had a friend with money, Carlos, who might help me. At the time, they didn't seem to care, but I kept negotiating with them and now it was paying off.

They brought me paper and pen, and I began to write. I told my friend I needed him to loan me money equal to the cost of my apartment and car. I told him he could have the apartment and car or I'd sell them and pay him back once I was home.

I asked him to please, please help me.

As I wrote, I underlined "the apartment" and "the car" many times.

"Why are you doing that?" the boss asked. He seemed agitated.

"So Carlos can understand," I said.

In my mind, I hoped Carlos would take the letter to my family and they would understand to ONLY pay the price of the apartment and the car, nothing more. I had discussed the price with my kidnappers, and I didn't want my family to pay more than what we agreed on.

It was a short letter, containing only what needed to be said.

"When is it going to be sent?" I asked, handing the letter to the boss.

"Probably today," he said.

"I hope it gets resolved soon," I said aloud, more to myself than him.

I spent many more days alone and sad, with the same routine: breakfast, lunch, and dinner.

But Henry started coming to visit more and more. He told me about how he got involved in kidnapping and how the organization worked.

Then we started getting more intimate with our conversations, talking about personal things. We got closer and closer. I needed someone to confide in, and it seemed he was really starting to care about me.

One night when he brought dinner, I asked, "Are you going to stay with me? Can you keep me company?"

"Yeah, why not?" he said. He stayed until I finished eating.

I asked, "Are you going to come later so we can talk some more?"

"I'm not supposed to, but I'm going to do it," he told me.

We continued our conversation that evening. I asked him why he wore clothes covering his arms and if he had a tattoo or mark on his body that he didn't want me to see.

"No. We don't want the kidnapped people to see us," he said.

"OK," I said, dropping it. It was a vague answer, but I didn't want to ask too much and make him suspicious.

I put my head on his shoulder, and he hugged me again.

Then I said, "I would like something from you."

"What?" he asked.

"I'd like you to give me a kiss," I said boldly.

Even though I was in a horrible situation, I felt safe with him. I knew I could control him, at least a little bit. I wasn't even afraid of his gun. Since this was what he seemed to want, too, I knew he wouldn't be suspicious or think I was trying to trick him.

"A kiss?" he asked, stunned.

"Yes, you don't feel the same?" I asked, using a very seductive voice.

"Yes, but not in this condition," he said, shaking his head.

"Condition? No one is looking at us here," I said.

"To give you a kiss, I have to remove my mask."

"You can pull it down or pull the mask up just enough so you can kiss," I suggested.

I was in seduction mode.

He pulled the mask up and gave me a kiss. It was a quick kiss, not a full kiss. More than a peck. I was disappointed. He was more nervous than me.

I liked the way it felt and said, "Oh, that's too short."

He was sitting with me, but he still had his gun resting between his legs.

I asked, "Are you afraid?"

"No."

"Then why was that kiss so quick?" I asked. "Why don't you give me another one, a little longer?"

He pulled his mask up a little more and kissed me again. It felt like a very long kiss, the longest kiss I ever had.

I don't know if it was really that long or if it was just the feeling of being touched after spending two months in isolation. I hadn't had real human contact in so long. It was a very, very big deal.

I felt aroused and wanted more from him, but he got a little afraid and said, "I have to go out."

"Go where?" I asked. I didn't want him to leave yet. Not now that we'd made this physical connection.

"Well, there are other guys out there, and I don't want them to get suspicious of what we are doing," he reminded me.

"Can we have a time where we are completely alone and see what happens?"

"Well, we need to plan that. There are always guards out there, but I can make that happen," Henry assured me.

"When?" I pressed.

"Let's see through the week when we can do it," he suggested.

He started coming every day, more and more often. We didn't always kiss, even though I asked him all the time. Sometimes he told me he couldn't. I didn't like that, but I could tell I had him wrapped around my finger.

I'd say, "Please, please, just a little kiss."

And he'd give in. We had mutual attraction and maybe even a kind of love. I didn't know if it was real or not, but at the time it felt real. I might have convinced myself it was real so that I could make it through the ordeal.

One day, the man who brought me lunch wasn't Henry.

"The other guy is taking a break. He'll be back to bring you dinner," he said gruffly.

Oh my God, he was going to come that night. I got really excited.

Henry came by to say, "I think we're going to be alone tonight."

"Alone, alone, alone?" I asked excitedly.

"Yes, alone. The other guys are going to go out, and I told them not to worry, that I'd stay with you," he said.

"Are you for sure?" I asked, almost unable to believe it.

"Yes."

"Well, you know I need to take a shower and everything, right?" I asked.

"Yeah, I know. Don't worry," Henry said.

I took a shower that day, so happy that I'd get alone time with him. That night, he came and closed the door completely.

"There's nobody here?" I asked.

"No," he confirmed.

"Are you for real?" I asked, still unable to believe it. I'd planned this carefully, and it was finally happening.

He started kissing me with his mask on but rolled it up his face. We were kissing, kissing, kissing. Then we started touching, caressing, and groping. I felt a lot of things I hadn't felt in what seemed like forever.

As we became more intimate, I asked, "Will you remove your mask? I can't see you in the darkness, and nobody is here."

He was a little afraid to do it, but then his emotions got the better of him. The feeling in that moment was more powerful than what he was supposed to be doing. His excitement was too high.

I removed his mask and then he was on top of me. He still had his clothes on. He never took his clothes off completely. I didn't know why, but I guessed it was so he could be ready to leave or could quickly get dressed if anyone came back.

I pulled his pants down a little, and he continued kissing me.

I touched his face and hair. He had very thin, fine hair. And his face was a little square and bony. I couldn't see his features in the dark, so I never did find out what he really looked like.

We were intimate and, in that moment, I loved him. I felt safe with him. I wanted him. At the time, those emotions felt real.

It wasn't the last time we were intimate, either. The next time, when I asked him to remove his mask, his emotions got the better of him, and he threw it off willingly.

When we were finished, he stayed with me.

"That was amazing," he said.

After that, things started changing for me. I got better food. More showers. Everything was on time. I wasn't waiting to be fed or taken care of.

It was a trauma response, and I couldn't blame myself for doing anything I needed to do to preserve my sanity and survive.

It was about taking control of the situation. He represented the potential for freedom.

A couple of days after I sent the letter to my friend, the boss came in and said, "Did you know your friend isn't going to pay?"

"How come? Did you hear from him?" I asked, worried.

"No, we talked to your father. He went to your friend, and your friend said he was scared and not going to help. Your father called and told us," he said.

I was devastated all over again. The second person I'd reached out to wasn't going to help either.

"I'll write to Clara, my best friend. She has a little bit of money and maybe she would help out," I said, giving him another option.

"OK, just do it, right now!" he ordered.

I told her everything that happened, asking her to please help. It was another short and precise letter. I was starting to wonder if there was anyone on the outside who could or would help me. It made me feel even more isolated and alone. I kept reaching out to people I thought I could trust, and they left me to suffer every time.

The kidnappers mailed the letter that same day.

I never heard anything about it. I kept asking what was going to happen. They kept telling me they were still thinking.

Were they thinking of killing me, selling me, or contacting my family again? They wouldn't tell me. I was alone in my little room with too many questions and no answers. Anxiety and depression ruled my life.

One day, the boss came in. "Why don't you contact your family again? Your friend sent the letter to your father, and your father contacted us again."

Later, I found out that the kidnappers called Clara's mother. It proved they'd been watching me for some time and knew who my friends were. They told her mom that they sent a letter to Clara and told her where she could find the letter, then hung up.

Clara's mother must have been nervous that kidnappers had her number and could probably track them. She called Clara, and together they must have called my father and told him about the letter.

My father went to get it. It was a big risk, but the boss eventually told me that my father had decided to open negotiations.

Meanwhile, I spent Christmas and New Year's in captivity. I could hear fireworks and cried because I couldn't share them with my daughter.

Some people who have experienced trauma are triggered by certain dates and events. I knew that if I was released, I would feel grateful for my life and freedom every Christmas I got to spend with her.

I told the boss that I was happy negotiations had started. "It's amazing. That probably means I'll get to go soon, right?"

I was getting a little ahead of myself, but I couldn't help it. I'd been a hostage for two-and-a-half months.

"We don't know. We just started talking and don't know how long he is going to take."

"What kind of things did you ask him?" I asked.

"We can't tell you," the boss said.

I could tell from his short, gruff answers that he was getting annoyed with my questions.

I felt anxious, in a good way. My family was talking to the kidnappers. Maybe they changed their minds or they had time to get the money. My father was a good businessman, so he would close the deal fast.

I was trying not to overthink the situation or burn myself out with worry. I wanted more news because I was moving closer and closer to freedom. It felt like the days were dragging on forever.

The only thing I wanted the minute I was released was to hold my daughter again.

I got tired of asking when they would let me go, and I released my anxiety, worry, and control to God. I asked Him for peace and patience. I surrendered to the situation.

That is when miracles can happen.

One day, I heard the sound of paper foil and packing or unpacking. I'd gotten used to listening for new sounds. I covered my mouth and cupped my ears so I could hear better.

I immediately sensed it was my captors counting money. But when would I be free?

I was so anxious, I couldn't sleep. I just couldn't wait until morning, when they brought me breakfast and I could ask when I was going home.

I tossed and turned, walked around, sat up and then laid down. My legs were restless. It was the longest night I'd ever experienced.

Henry brought breakfast, and I jumped up out of bed. I knew I could ask him anything because he'd be nice. By that point, we'd been intimate several times.

"You guys got the money," I said.

"How did you know?" he asked.

"I heard you counting it last night. Don't lie to me at this point. We've shared a lot. Don't lie to me."

He said, "Yeah, we got the money."

I hugged him.

"Please, calm down. No one can know that you know this. Don't worry, you'll get out soon," he promised.

"How soon?"

"We need to prepare the area before we release you so there are no cops, no GAULA, and the place is clean," he said. "We don't want them to follow us."

"How long will that take?" I asked, still excited and anxious.

"Two days to a week."

I was disheartened. "How come? You got the money. Open the

67

door for me, and I'll go."

"It isn't like that," he said. "You just need to wait."

Everything seemed to be in slow motion. My mind invented all kinds of stuff. I was brushing my hair with my fingers, asking to stay a little longer in the shower, and doing exercises in my room. I did anything I could do to pass the time more quickly.

The days were longer than ever.

Three days later, Henry brought me breakfast and whispered, "Guess what?"

"What?" I asked before touching my food.

"You're going to get released today. But be quiet, there are a lot of people outside," he said.

I nearly burst out of my body; I was so excited! This was the moment I was waiting for. It was a moment I didn't know would ever come! I could barely contain myself, despite still being locked in a room with my kidnapper.

"When do I go?" I asked excitedly.

"Later at night," he said.

"At night?" That seemed like an eternity from now. "Where will you leave me?"

"Downtown."

"No, no, no, please don't leave me downtown." I grabbed his arm delicately. "Please, for everything that happened between us and the love you have for me, please leave me in a place where I will be safe."

The downtown area where I lived was famous for being danger-ous at night. Women alone could get mugged, raped, kidnapped, beaten, or murdered. The area was dark and quiet because it was all stores and businesses. No one lived there, so there was no one to call for help. No one wanted to go there alone at night, espe-cially not women.

"Don't worry, I'm going to help you with this."

I couldn't wait to get out of there, but that last day was so long! I knocked on the door, asking the time. It was 10 a.m. When they gave me lunch, it was only noon.

Later, I knocked again, asking the time. The men outside my door kept telling me, "No, not yet."

"If you knock one more time, we aren't going to release you today. Behave," one man said.

I decided to be quiet and pray that I would be safe.

At 10 p.m., Henry came in, all dressed up. The men had to try to look different so they wouldn't be suspicious.

"Are you ready?" he asked.

"I'm super ready to go." I couldn't wait to hold my daughter.

There were more people outside the room. I asked him to close the door, and he did. I hugged him. He hugged me back, the strongest hug I've ever had in my life.

"OK, it's time to go. But you have to behave," he said. "I'm not going to cover your eyes because I trust you. Keep your eyes closed."

"You think at this point, I'll do something to risk my freedom?" I asked.

They put me in the car but not the trunk. I sat in the back seat with two other people. I think it was a taxi because it would look less suspicious having one driver with everyone else in the back seat.

Henry put his arm around me to keep me from moving.

"I am so glad to have met you. I'm happy that you're getting released, and I'm sad I'll never see you again. I wish I didn't meet you in this situation," Henry whispered to me. "I have your beeper number. In seven days, I will message you to let you know that I still remember you."

"OK." But I really didn't want him to message me.

Before taking me from the room, he gave me some cash—for a payphone and for a taxi if the payphone didn't work. Henry said he didn't want anything to happen to me ever again.

Sometimes, criminal groups in Colombia know about individuals who have been kidnapped. When one is released, it means a ransom was paid, so a new group moves in to rekidnap the former hostage all over again.

"Please get out of the car and walk as fast as you can to a payphone or taxi, whatever you see first," Henry said. "Call your family and go home. Don't even say to the taxi driver that you've been released."

"Can you please tell me where I am, so I don't get disoriented?" I asked.

"It is where you asked me to be released," he assured me.

He opened the door, and I got out. There was a brick wall, and I stood against it.

"Don't turn around for ten minutes," he said.

I don't know how long I stood facing the wall. I was disoriented by my freedom. It could have been 10 seconds or 10 years for all I knew.

I walked right to a payphone, but I couldn't remember the number to my house or how to dial. I got anxious about what Henry said about being re-kidnapped, so I got a taxi.

"Take me to my home," I blurted out.

"What? Where is home?" he asked. I hadn't even given him the address.

"I'm not feeling well. Can you drive, and I'll direct you?" I asked, still too dazed to think clearly.

When the taxi pulled in front of my parents' condo, I saw dozens of men, private security, waiting for me. My dad took me out of the taxi and right away into the apartment. He stared at me in shock. I didn't know why at first, but he seemed confused by the way I looked. All the money the kidnappers gave me, I gave to the taxi driver. I don't know how much the fare was, but I gave it all to him.

The police pulled him from the cab.

"No, no, no! He's just a taxi driver," I said.

They must have thought he was one of the kidnappers. In a kidnap situation, every person is a suspect until they can find the true ones.

My two brothers weren't there with the rest of my family. They were still in Canada, where my father had sent them.

My daughter was the first to say anything. "Mommy, Mommy, Mommy, you're not going to go anywhere, are you?"

I hugged her really tightly. With her in my arms, I felt happy and peaceful. I couldn't let her go, and she clung to me just as tightly.

Finally, I was home!

Chapter 6

DAD DOESN'T BELIEVE ME

When I saw my daugh-
ter, all I could do was
hug her. I was so happy to
see her again. I cried and
cried, unable to believe that
I was really home.

There were 40 or 50 other
people in my parents' house
with a mariachi band and
tons of food for celebration.
There were flowers every-
where, maybe 70 different bouquets.

It was a wish come true that I was there. For months, I'd been
wondering if I'd ever see my daughter again. Finally, I had my
freedom, and I was able to hold her in my arms. It was the only
thing I wanted in that moment.

For the three months that I was kidnapped, my daughter had been my anchor. She was the one that kept me going and gave me the determination to survive and get out. If she didn't exist when I heard my father refuse to pay the ransom, I would have given up. It was my daughter who kept me going.

I hugged my father and my mother and everyone else. I still felt resentment toward my parents about what they had said on the phone.

I'd carried that resentment through a huge chunk of the kidnapping. I wasn't as excited to see them as I was to see my daughter or as happy to be free because of that feeling.

They sat me down and tried to get me to eat.

I didn't want to eat. I really just wanted things to be quiet.

It was very loud with the mariachi music and lots of chatter from the guests. Mariachis are common at celebrations in Colombia and to my family, this was a big celebration. My father even dedicated a song to me—*Es Mi Nina Bonita*, which means My Beautiful Girl.

I cried a lot and felt very emotional. I also noticed everyone staring at me. It made me uncomfortable because it seemed like they couldn't believe I'd come back, and I looked as healthy as I did before.

How had I managed to look so good after spending three months in the dark without sun or fresh air? My skin was a little paler, but I'd eaten the food because I knew it would keep me alive.

I had tried to do some exercise in the little room, but I couldn't get the cardio going. I'm a petite woman, and I gained about five pounds while in captivity. For my size, that was a noticeable amount of weight, and my cheeks were round and puffy. People said I looked like an angel.

My father said in front of everyone, "Well, you don't look like you were kidnapped."

I received that message in a very different way. It sounded like my father was accusing me of orchestrating my own kidnapping to get money from my family. I knew that this sometimes happened.

Upset, I went to my mother, who was in another room.

"What the fuck is wrong with Father?" I asked her. "I just got back, and he's saying I don't look like I've been kidnapped. Why do you think I would kidnap myself?"

"Oh, you're going to start again," she said dismissively.

"No, I just got back from being kidnapped. I thought all you and he would do is hug me and give me kisses and tell me you missed me," I said.

I remembered telling the kidnappers I hoped my family would appreciate me more because I never felt like they'd loved me enough and always took me for granted. Everyone was partying and drinking, but I was upset, so I went to my room and slept. But before I closed my eyes, I made a decision: I'm going to move to the United States.

That first night of freedom, I cried myself to sleep, just like I did the night I'd been kidnapped. At least this time, my daughter slept in bed with me.

I was overwhelmed with a lot of emotions: happiness, sadness, anxiety, and excitement. I was also afraid and felt guilty because of the emotional connection I had to Henry, one of my kidnappers. I worried about what would happen if my family found out.

I couldn't tell them what had happened and how well I had been treated, because they'd take it the wrong way. They'd act like I hadn't been kidnapped—that I'd been part of a scam and helped arrange my own kidnapping.

The worst part was, I felt like I'd done something wrong having had an emotional connection to Henry. I wound up hiding that secret for 17 years. I even told Henry that our connection was something I'd never talk about, and it would die with me. I felt ashamed.

For several years, I didn't understand this feeling or what it meant or why I felt it. At the time, I didn't know about Stockholm Syndrome, and I couldn't make sense of my feelings and thoughts.

Looking back, I wish I had counseling immediately after my release. My family weren't well educated in trauma and how it might affect me, so they never brought me to a therapist. I suffered, holding onto what happened with Henry while I was in captivity and trying to sort through it on my own.

My family avoided the topic of my kidnapping. They probably felt a lot of the same things I felt, like guilt and fear. They probably didn't know about Stockholm Syndrome, either.

As much as I wanted to, I learned quickly that I couldn't just snap back into my old life and pick up where I left off.

The morning after the celebration, I woke up and a man who worked in our house brought breakfast to my bedroom.

"How was it? How are you feeling? Are you OK?" he asked me.

I started crying. He was the first person to ask me if I was OK. He knew how bad things were for me living with my parents before I was kidnapped. He knew all the secrets in the family because he saw everything.

He talked to me and hugged me and that made me happy.

After breakfast, I had my first warm shower in three months. I spent almost an hour in the shower thinking about my freedom and the possibility of moving to the US.

I didn't have any clothes at my parent's house because I had my own apartment. Over lunch with my parents and some of their friends, I told them I'd like to go back to my apartment to collect my things.

"Apartment, what apartment?" my dad asked.

"The apartment you gave me. The one I had before I was kid-napped," I said.

Sarcastically, my dad responded, "How do you think I paid for your kidnapping?"

"So, you're telling me that I paid for my kidnapping?" I asked, a little shocked.

"No, I gave you that apartment. I paid," he said.

I learned that they packed all my stuff up into boxes and put them into storage. I asked my father to take everything out of storage, and he said something sarcastic again. I snapped and left the table.

I didn't want to leave my room. My bedroom was at least three times the size of the room in which I'd been held captive, and there was a giant picture window next to the bed.

I opened the window, breathing in the fresh air. Everything looked more vibrant. They'd released me at night, so I hadn't seen much on the drive home. The only thing I remembered was getting a taxi. Now the world looked brighter and more beautiful.

I was mesmerized.

I learned from being kidnapped that every little detail is important, and I've since spent hours observing the nature around me. The way I saw the world had changed for the better.

I mostly stayed in my room for the next few days and had meals brought to me. Even though I was free, I didn't feel like much had changed, except for the daily visits from the GAULA agents.

DAD DOESN'T BELIEVE ME

One particular agent came by every day and asked me the same questions.

He asked, "Did you know where you were?"

"No."

"Did you see any faces?"

"No."

"Can you describe heights and weights?"

I described the heights and weights of my kidnappers and what I thought their ages were.

"Did you see their faces?"

"No."

"Who did you talk to regularly?"

"One or two, sometimes three of them."

"Did you hear any noises outside—traffic, nature, voices, etc.?"

"I don't know. I heard two women talking on the second floor, but I don't know if they were part of the group."

"Here are pictures. Do you recognize any of them?"

"No. How would I if I didn't see their faces?"

"How did they talk?"

"Normally."

"Did they have high education or low education?"

"In the middle. They had different levels of education."

He stayed for an hour or hour-and-a-half every day for three months. He talked to me slowly, not pushing. He watched for all my reactions, observing how I spoke and how I acted.

After seeing the same pictures over and over again, I became frustrated and threw the pictures back at him.

"If you'd done your job in the first place, I wouldn't have been kidnapped!" I shouted. "What does it matter now? I'm back!"

Despite my frustration, I began to feel fond of him. He was the only one checking on me regularly. I felt reliant on him for the emotional support I wasn't getting from my family.

It was through him that I discovered the response my parents gave during the radio call was directed by the GAULA, which specialized in hostage situations. GAULA specialized in solving hostage-taking situations. Founded in 1996, they were an elite unit dedicated to fighting kidnapping and extortion, meaning they were exactly the people I wanted working on my case.

For them, telling my parents to respond that way was a valid strategy that often works because the kidnapper doesn't know what to do. It helped them buy time and distract the kidnappers while they got the money. I didn't know that at the time. Instead, I felt a complete lack of love.

My daughter, who was only a couple of years old, was very attached to me. She never wanted to leave me or go anywhere without me. She was clearly afraid of losing me again.

On the other hand, my parents were more disconnected and didn't seem to be affected by my trauma. I never talked to them about it, and they never asked me how I was, how I felt or anything about what I was going through.

It wasn't that they didn't love me or that they didn't understand the situation. They just didn't know how to talk to me or look after my mental health.

Only my aunt in Canada spoke up, telling my mother, "She needs to get help."

My mother said, "Yeah, yeah." But she didn't know what kind of "help" to get me.

"I want you to send her to Canada. She's going to get political asylum, help from the government, and therapy," my aunt said.

My parents asked me if I wanted to go, and I said no. I lived in Canada the first seven years of my life but didn't remember anything about it. I wanted to go to the United States.

I started listening to salsa music in my room, especially a love song that Henry told me would always remind him of me. My kidnappers played a lot of salsa, probably to keep me from hearing outside noises.

The GAULA agent wanted me to keep my beeper with me as a way to trace any messages. Before releasing me, Henry said he had my beeper number and would see me again. I didn't want to see him again, but I still tried to hold onto our connection.

I didn't tell the agent that one of the kidnappers said he'd contact me, but he might have suspected that I had Stockholm Syndrome and would try to contact them.

He might also have had other cases where kidnappers reached out to their victims after their release. I kept the beeper with me, feeling anxious whenever I got a new message.

Henry said he would send me a text a week after I was released, so I would know he was thinking of me and that he wanted to see me again.

I counted the days. I felt nervous and didn't know what would happen if my family found out.

Exactly one week later, the beeper rang with an unknown number, and I knew it was Henry. My heart raced when I saw it, but I realized I didn't love him. My emotional connection to him wasn't real.

I used him to help me escape. I didn't want to see him ever again, and I wanted to leave the country altogether.

That was easier said than done. My parents kept a very close eye on me. I was never allowed to leave their home.

For the first seven days after I was released, I didn't leave my bedroom, except to shower and eat. They wouldn't even let me bring my own daughter to school.

The college in which I had been enrolled before I was kidnapped had a peace march to celebrate my release. It was another celebration for me, but I couldn't go to that either.

Slowly, I felt like I was starting to wake up. The college director called my parents and told them he wanted to talk to me. Finally, two weeks after my release, my father told me I had to go to school and get back into my old life.

I was excited because it was finally a chance for me to get out of the house and do something outside the routine I'd been stuck in—again. I was also a little afraid because I would be following the same route as the day I was kidnapped.

I needn't have worried. My father sent me with three bodyguards, but it was difficult for me to pass the familiar streets.

The director hugged me and was very happy to see me.

"You almost finished your third semester. We want you to skip your classes and take a test. If you pass, you'll move onto the next semester," he said.

Part of me was happy and grateful that the college director wanted me back, but I couldn't just fall back into my old life like nothing happened. I thanked him but declined the offer. It was surreal—and suffocating—being back in the place where I'd been kidnapped.

The school felt different, too. It no longer felt safe or like a place where I could learn or wanted to be.

I never truly wanted to study a career in business administration. My father made me to do it. If I had refused, he would not have financially supported me anymore, and at the time, I had a child and no money.

I spent most of my time with my daughter. I was happy to be with her again, but I was also very, very sad and confused. I cried and even missed Henry a little.

The hardest part was that I'd gained my freedom, but I still didn't feel free. I wasn't allowed to go out by myself, see friends, or ever have any privacy. Even when I was alone in my room, people were always standing nearby, coming into my room to check on me, and hovering around, watching me.

My parents essentially turned my home into another prison. I knew it was because they were afraid for me and didn't want me to get taken again, but it was like my own family had kidnapped me!

Three months after being released, I was going crazy in my parents' house. I asked my father if I could see a friend.

This was a new friend of mine, whom I hadn't spent a lot of time with yet. It was such a relief to see her, and I was glad my dad agreed. Of course, he sent people to keep an eye on me.

The bodyguards waited outside my friend's apartment building while I went inside. I knew they'd still be there when I came back out.

From the second floor, where my friend lived, I heard a very noisy car with loud music. I wondered who it was, so I looked over the balcony and saw an attractive man.

He's going to be my husband, I thought. He looked up and saw me, too. He lived across the hall from my friend, and he came up to say hello to her. He stared at me for a while.

There was an instant soul connection. I'd seen Henry as a way to help me out of the kidnapping situation. I saw this man, whose name was Edy, as a way to escape my father.

"I want to take you out," Edy said.

"I can't. My parents won't let me go anywhere," I explained.

"I don't care. I like you. I want to take you out," he insisted.

I really liked his confidence and forwardness. He was willing to take control and get what he wanted.

Because of my father's strict rules, I couldn't see Edy a lot, but he still pursued me. After three months of barely seeing each other, he finally gave me the way out I had hoped for.

"I can't stand it anymore. I want to marry you because it is the only way I can see you. I'm in love with you," he said.

"You'll have to call my father and ask for my hand," I said.

Even though I saw him as my escape, I never played with his emotions. I thought I really loved him.

Edy asked my father's permission to marry me. Afterward, my father came to talk to me and told me what happened.

"Do you want to marry him?" he asked.

"Yes, I do!"

"I like that he came to me and talked to me first. He's a nice guy, and I approve of him."

We got married a week later. I picked out a blue wedding dress for myself, and we said our vows before his family and my father. My mother couldn't make it because she was traveling, and I didn't want to wait for her.

As a wife, I was loyal and loved him because I relied on him for my freedom. I started feeling more secure right away. Because of the business he was in, he had private security that I knew would keep me safe as his wife.

I was like a chameleon, turning into what I needed to survive whatever situation I was in. It was easy for me to get attached to anyone I met after the kidnapping. I instantly felt like I needed them.

Even though my father approved of my husband, he continued to try and control me. My parents also tried to use my daughter as a way to control me.

My husband noticed and asked me what we were going to do about it.

Nine months after we married, I told him I wanted to move to the US.

"Are you staying or are you coming?" I asked.

I had to get away from my parents, and with my kidnappers still at large in Colombia, I didn't feel safe.

"I'm going with you," he said.

"You can find a place and work for a month, and then I'll come join you and work," I said.

"You've never had a job before."

"That's OK," I said. "We're going to do what we have to in order to make this work."

LIVING IN THE U.S.A.

While we were getting ready to move to the US, my mother got sick. She was in the hospital, and I didn't want to leave until she got better. My life felt like it was on hold.

But she wasn't getting any better, and when I visited her in the hospital, she told me to go ahead and move.

"Do this for yourself," she said. "Go and be happy."

I didn't need her permission, but getting her blessing made a huge difference. I left the hospital feeling a lot lighter and happier. My life could finally start.

My husband left first for New York City. He got us a garage apartment and got a job at a car wash. A month later, it was time for me to join him.

My father was very calm when I told him I was leaving the country.

His expression didn't change at all as he said, "You can't come to me for help like you did when you were kidnapped. I won't support you."

I understood that he was actually very upset. He knew that once I left the country with my daughter, we'd be beyond his reach.

I felt like I was being disowned. My father couldn't keep me at home and control me, so he was punishing me in whatever way they could for following my own path.

The day I left, I discovered who really cared about me. No one in my family came to the airport. My father's worker, who brought the money for my rescue, gave me a ride and was the only one there. I also found out he was the person who made the ransom drop. By GAULA organization rules, the family can't do that.

He walked into the airport with me and put his arm around me.

"I'm glad you're doing this," he said. "You're doing the right thing for yourself."

I had one suitcase and $500 in my pocket. When I packed up, I left all my nice clothes and other things behind. I wondered if displaying my wealth was one of the reasons I was targeted by the kidnappers.

I took a taxi from the airport to the garage apartment, and the taxi driver and I got to talking. I told him a little about my situation, and he offered to help me find a job since I didn't have all my papers yet.

I appreciated the offer, but I didn't expect him to follow up with me.

I was so excited to be in the US! Even though I didn't have a job or support from my family, I felt like this was right and that everything would work out. When you're living in alignment, good things come to you.

At first, my husband was nervous for me to see our new home, a $500-a-month apartment in Queens on Liberty Street. What a street name to start with—Liberty! The teeny, tiny efficiency was nothing like the large and extravagant accommodation in which I'd grown up.

I left a life of wealth for one that was much more modest, and Edy was worried that I wouldn't be happy because the change was too drastic.

I told him I could overcome anything because I didn't want to feel kidnapped by my own family. Freedom was what I wanted. I absolutely loved the little garage apartment. I didn't need fancy clothes or a nice car. I wanted to live my own life.

The best part was we'd gotten it all on our own without my father's help. This wasn't something that he could hold over my head someday.

I was surprised when the taxi driver showed up the next day to make good on his offer to help find me a job. It just reaffirmed for me that I was on the right path. I'd been in the US for less than 24 hours, and all the pieces were already falling into place.

I was excited to work because I'd never had a job before. I really wanted to help support my lifestyle and my family and make my own way.

The taxi driver brought me to a hardware store, where I spoke to the owner and was hired on the spot. Unfortunately, it was only a part-time job, and I wanted to work more than that.

We didn't have a car yet, so I walked to and from my new job. On the walk home, I decided I was going to get a second part-time job for the afternoons and manifested that. Door by door, I knocked on every single business all the way down the street.

"Are you hiring?" I asked over and over again until my head was spinning.

It was a very cold day, and I was exhausted and my feet hurt. No one had any part-time work for me, until I got to the very last door on the street.

I'd heard "no" so many times while I was kidnapped that I didn't care if I heard it again. What did I have to lose by going through that last door and asking for a job? It was a carpet store, and they had a part-time job with afternoon hours, just like I wanted!

Again, I felt all the affirmation I needed that I was moving in the right direction.

As much as I loved my new life, I didn't like New York. I didn't like the cold, and I didn't like having to walk everywhere. I really missed my daughter, too, but I knew she couldn't move into the little efficiency apartment with us.

I decided that I wanted to move to Florida. We got a real-estate agent and started looking for apartments in Orlando. Our new apartment was only $550 a month and twice the size of our place in New York.

By then, we had managed to save $3,000 for the move. My husband assumed that we were going to fly to Orlando.

I said, "No. We need to be smart with the money because we are starting again in a new place."

"How will we get there?" he asked.

"By train, Dear, in twenty-four hours," I said.

Within a few days of moving, I got a job at a carpet store with my experience from New York. A gas station right across the street was owned by the same woman, and she gave me a job there, too.

The neighborhood we lived in, and where I worked, wasn't the best neighborhood. One night while I was working at the gas station, a group of men came in just to get a pack of gum. They didn't say anything to me, but I felt threatened. Maybe I was a little paranoid, but that same day, I resigned.

Thinking back, I think being kidnapped made me more sensitive to people around me. Before that, a few guys buying a pack of gum wouldn't have rattled me so much.

But the very next day, the owner called me to say that the gas station had been robbed and her brother locked in the bathroom. I was glad I listened to my intuition.

While I was kidnapped, my daughter was my anchor. When I came to the US, I couldn't bring her with me right away. I needed to get settled in.

Now that we were in Orlando, it was time to get her. I had a modest room with dolls and stuffed animals. Everything was used, but I decorated the room just for her.

When I told my mom I wanted my daughter to join me in the US, my mom said, "No. I don't want her living there. The way you live, I don't want her living like that."

One of the reasons we came to the US was to get away from my family using my daughter to control me. They were still trying to do it.

Furious, I said, "She's my daughter. She has to live with me, no matter where I am."

After a lot of arguing with my mother, I convinced her to bring my daughter to me in Florida. We had been there eight months. At first, I was worried about what she would think about the room I decorated for her. It was smaller and much different than her fancy room in Colombia.

When she saw her new room, she lit right up and said, "Oh, Mommy, I love this room. I love it so much."

It made me so happy to have her back and to know she loved what I could offer her. She was six years old at the time.

I also enrolled my daughter in school. Since I had to work so many hours, she was in after-school care a lot. It was really rough, and I wasn't as present in her life as I wanted to be.

Meanwhile, I was still waiting for my work visa and asylum papers when I heard about a job at a blueberry company. I had no idea when the papers would come, only that I needed them to be hired.

I went for an interview anyway, and they wanted to hire me but couldn't.

"When you get your papers, this job will be waiting for you if we still have an opening," the interviewer said.

I left feeling hopeful and when I arrived home, my papers were in the mailbox. I turned right around the next day, went to the blueberry company, and showed them my papers. I was hired immediately.

I did so well in the first 48 hours that my manager, Jack, offered me a promotion with a raise from $5.25 an hour to $7.50.

Since everything was working out, I felt like I didn't have to worry about my past. It seemed like I'd left the kidnapping behind in Colombia, and it couldn't touch me anymore.

I was so happy to get that raise so quickly and knew at that moment I was going for more. I saw the person in charge of quality control—his name was Jay—and what he was doing looked very easy, so I asked him if he could teach me. He replied, "No I cant, you need to talk to my boss and see if he can teach you!" I said OK!

The next day I saw Jay's boss and asked him if he could teach me quality control and he said, "Well, you need to study to be a professional on doing quality control."

I said, "Where can I go to be a professional on quality control?"

He said, "You need to go to Winter Heaven in Orlando, it's like forty-five minutes away, and go to the US Department of Agriculture (USDA) and apply for quality control inspector."

The next day I had my day off. I went to pick up the application and when I got there, an old lady that was in the receptionist told me, "Oh, my dear! You are so lucky. Today, the regional manager who hires people for USDA is here. Do you want to come in today and do the interview?"

"What!? I'm in jeans and not dressed up for an interview," I said, panicking.

"Don't worry," she assured me. "You'll be fine!"

After a two-hour interview, the regional manager told me I would be hired when they had openings. Then he put my application on top of the stack on his desk.

Soon after, someone from the USDA called to tell me they had a quality inspector position available for me. It came with a sizable raise, and I could start in October.

I was so excited!

At this time, I was making more money than my husband, Edy. I could support myself completely. When I thought of my ideal relationship, it was with a man who made more money than me and was a family provider.

I still hadn't recovered from my trauma. I felt like I needed someone to take care of me and provide for me in order to be safe. When Edy could no longer do that, I didn't feel safe, and my survival mode kicked in. I had to get away from him and find someone else.

When I told Edy I wanted a divorce, he was very upset. He kept telling me he loved me and tried to get me to stay with him. He wasn't mad or mean, just very sad and loving.

My mind was made up, however, and I was done. I told him that he had seven days to leave. Every single day, he told me he loved me, but I wouldn't listen. Even my mom tried to change my mind about leaving him when she was here for vacation.

Shortly after my divorce was finalized, I began a romantic relationship with Jay. When my mom found out about Jay, she got angry!

She called me a lot of names and even tried to slap me. I grabbed her hand and told her never to do that again. I made her leave my home, too. She called Edy and he came to pick her up. I thought it was incredibly disrespectful for her to continue manipulating my life.

Around the same time, I decided I wanted to leave Orlando and move to Miami. Jay and I agreed to go together, and he offered me a position there. I'd also be getting a very sizable pay increase.

We lived together, but we didn't get married. I was still jumping from man to man. Because of the trauma I'd gone through, I saw men as a pillar of stability and support. They were a means to freedom and safety, whether or not they actually provided that.

THE SPARK

When I worked in the produce industry with Jay, I was exposed to a lot of chemicals, so I made the decision not to have any more children. I didn't want to risk it. But sometimes, what we want isn't what happens, and I ended up getting pregnant.

Due to my limited health insurance, I didn't go for a prenatal appointment or my first ultrasound until I was five months pregnant. The ultrasound revealed that my daughter, Maria Antonia, had a cleft lip and leg deformities and water in her brain.

"What does that mean?" I asked the doctors.

The doctor explained that the limb deformities could be fixed surgically, but they said she'd have permanent brain damage. They recommended that I terminate the pregnancy.

As horrifying as that sounded, I knew it was the right thing to do. It was a reminder of why I had made the decision not to have more children.

They gave me 72 hours to decide. Those 72 hours were terrible. I couldn't sleep. I felt guilt and shame about the decision I needed to make. I wanted to scream to the entire world, why me—again!?

I remember going to the hospital feeling very sad. I undressed and put on a hospital gown. After I laid down, the doctor explained to me what he was going to do. He also asked me to not look at the monitor during the procedure. But I did.

The doctor injected her directly in the heart with potassium chloride. I watched on the ultrasound screen. As awful as it was, I wanted to see the process. I was putting her through this. At first, her little heart beat so fast and frantically. I felt nauseous and guilty. It is something that I will never forget.

Then her heart began slowing. That was the most pain I ever felt, though I did the best I could for both of us. I was induced next, but I couldn't push her out. I pushed and pushed for 24 hours, but she wouldn't come. There was nothing else the doctors could do.

They sent me home and said the tissue will come out on its own. For seven days, I carried her around. There was no movement, no life. I saw myself in the mirror and I felt like I was 100 years old. I didn't recognize myself. After a week, I couldn't take it anymore and went to the doctor again.

In the lobby, I made a huge scene, screaming at the nurses and doctors about what was happening inside of me. I was emotionally overwhelmed and distraught.

Finally, they admitted me and used a machine to pull the fetus out in small pieces. They were poking me and prodding me at a time when I didn't want to be touched at all. It was very violating and traumatic. I felt like dying with her. My heart was breaking into pieces.

I felt humiliation, abandonment, rejection, injustice, and betrayal—my childhood wounds all in one moment. I asked God, "Why do I need to experience this? Why do I have to go through these situations over and over when they are so traumatic for my soul? What exactly did I do in my past life for me to have all these experiences?!"

I left the hospital like a zombie. I didn't feel anything, and I told my mother that I didn't know who I was anymore.

After losing my baby, I went into a very deep, dark depression. I isolated myself from everyone, including Jay and my daughter. I never wanted to get up or get out of bed. I didn't want to leave my house or even my room.

I wasn't showering or taking care of myself. My state of mind and the mental and physical prison I'd created for myself were very similar to what I had experienced while I was kidnapped and when I was stuck at my parents' home.

Jay noticed my depression, but I don't think he knew how to help, not at first.

One day, he asked, "Do you want to come to Michigan with me? I have to go for work. Maybe changing your scenery will feel better."

When we got to Michigan, it was the same thing. I still slept a lot. I sat on the couch all day. I didn't want to do anything, and I cried all the time. I was a shell of my former self.

My daughter was eight years old by that time and could take care of herself. I wasn't paying much attention to her or interacting with her a lot. I was stuck in my own head and my own emotions. Depression can make it really hard to interact with other people, even those you love the most.

Every day, Jay would say, "Let's go for a walk. Let's do something."

And I would say, "I don't want to do anything."

One day, he came to me and said, "There are three bicycles outside. Do you want to go on a bicycle ride?"

Jay, my daughter, and I all got on the bicycles and went for a long ride through the neighborhood and park. For several hours, while I was out in the sun, getting exercise and with the people I loved, I felt better.

But as soon as we returned home, that happiness faded, and I was back in my depressive state.

Around this time, I began to discover art and painting. When I was in college, I always doodled in the edge of my notes. I didn't know why I was so drawn to art, but it fascinated me and brought my schoolwork to life.

It was around this time, however, that Jay started getting frustrated. He was also concerned about me. I wasn't really getting any better.

"How long are you going to be sitting down, crying, and dealing with your depression? You don't think you have to start working and doing something? This is too much for me," he said.

I took it all wrong. I felt humiliated for his calling me out like that. I felt like he didn't understand me or empathize with me. He was just telling me to get over it and move on so life would be easier for him.

At least, that's how I saw it. I immediately started screaming at him.

Now, I see it differently, of course. Since I've gone through the healing process, I understand he was giving me the push I needed. It wasn't what I wanted but it was something.

In that moment, however, my ego lashed out at him.

"You know what? You're fucking right. I'm going to show you how I can move on," I yelled.

Sometimes, it's hard to see that the people closest to you are giving you what you need. I was still living in survival mode—fight or flight—so I immediately started fighting when I heard something I didn't like. It triggered my past wounds from the traumas of my childhood and kidnapping. Fierce reactions to abandonment, rejection, humiliation, and injustice flooded out of me.

We returned to Miami, and my mission was to find a job and start living life again. I also decided that Jay was not the man for me. I still saw what he said to me as disrespectful. I didn't want a man who disrespected and humiliated me.

Our relationship hadn't been great before the trauma of losing our baby. I'd been thinking of leaving him before I got pregnant, but I stayed because of the baby.

It was more and more clear that we didn't understand each other, and he wasn't the one for me. I was still living with this fantasy that my "perfect" romance would be with a handsome man who made more money than me and understood me completely. In that idealized romance, we would never fight or argue.

It was truly a fantasy that I'd built for myself as a result of my Stockholm Syndrome. I saw that "perfect man" and "perfect relationship" as what I needed for support and stability. When someone fell short, I'd leave and fall right into the next relationship.

Even though I didn't appreciate what he said at the time, I can look back on it and thank him for pushing me out of my depression.

I became a single mother, but I made it work. Sometimes, I had to pick my daughter up from school and bring her to work with me. There were times I set her up in the office to do her homework because I was working late. As a quality control inspector, I knew the containers could come at any time, and I had to be there.

At times, she even had to sleep in the office because she was too young to stay home alone while I worked.

Sometimes, she had homework that I didn't understand. I told her all the time, just do what you can. I don't need you to be perfect. I just want you to pass your classes. She struggled because of an undiagnosed memory problem, but she pushed through and got a good education.

Part of what I realized after leaving Jay and struggling as a single mom was that I wasn't living my purpose or my dream in my current career. I started looking at what I wanted to do with the rest of my life. My entrepreneurial spirit was emerging, and I knew I didn't want to sit at a desk all day, working as a secretary or produce inspector. I wanted to create an import and wholesale produce business.

CONSTANT MOTION

Even though my career was taking off, I still faced some hardships.

Initially, I was in the US on visas and temporary papers. It took a long time for me to get my citizenship status, and at times, it seemed like the entire universe was against me.

I was continually worried that I would be deported back to the country where I was kidnapped.

Over the course of 11 years, I received three orders of deportation. I also applied for political asylum.

When I told my story to a judge in Miami, I explained the kidnapping and why I felt like I had to leave Colombia for my safety.

"Did your family pay a ransom for you?" the judge asked after I'd shown proof of my kidnapping.

"Yes."

"Then you can't have political asylum," she said.

"But if they hadn't paid, I wouldn't be here," I said.

"You can only get political asylum if you feel unsafe and are trying to escape," she said.

"I do feel unsafe. The kidnappers were never caught, and I don't want to stay there and get kidnapped again," I told her. "I needed to leave the country."

"I don't believe you."

My first attempt at getting residency was denied. I met with my immigration lawyer and asked, "How many times can I do this?"

"Three times. Let's go for the second time," he said.

I felt better about my second attempt. My lawyer and I had worked on the details of my case and my request for asylum. We came up with a new way to present it and tweaked the argument to reinforce that I would be in danger if I returned to my home country. I worked very hard with my lawyer to produce a better, stronger case for my second court date.

My second immigration appointment was set for September 12, 2001. When I stood before the judge at my immigration hearing one day after the World Trade Center tragedy, he wouldn't even listen to my story. It was a bad time to try and become a US citizen.

I went before immigration judges 15 times to pursue my citizenship, three of which resulted in a deportation order. Every single time, I was shaking in my boots, scared I would be thrown in handcuffs and sent back to Colombia.

If I was deported, it would mean facing my past, and I wasn't ready for that. I didn't have the right tools, and I didn't even know I had healing to do.

For me, living life in survival mode was like being in a constant adrenaline-fueled state. It was exhausting and wore me down.

I hit points where my body would literally give out, and I'd become very depressed. Once I "recovered," I went right back into survival mode.

For years, I was constantly on the move with my career, my citizenship, and my romantic relationships. Through the entire process, I had to deal with all kinds of emotions. There were very stressful times when all I could do was work to pay my bills and my lawyers. It was like I couldn't settle down or I'd be too vulnerable.

Of course, this was my trauma talking because I hadn't done what I needed to heal.

After my relationship with Jay ended, another man entered the picture. Allen and I had been together for a while when he said, "I'll marry you, and we can form a family." He knew my legal battles and wanted to help. We also loved each other very much.

His offer calmed my nerves, again. I married Allen, and I was able to get my citizenship. I was so happy that another miracle had happened for me and my daughter. The opportunity to stay in the USA, the country that I love the most and a haven for me and my daughter, was exciting and gave me relief.

Then, after 11 years, I got my residency papers and was able to become a full citizen of the United States. It was a true dream come true.

I was always working to make things happen.

I had to face a lot of injustice in the system. Being kidnapped for three months was not enough according to US immigration laws to get asylum, and my family paying to bring me home safely was grounds to deny asylum. The US courts concluded that my family was supporting crime by paying ransom, but what they didn't understand was that families in Colombia have to pay or their loved ones are killed.

Once I was married, the deportation orders were lifted. I no longer needed the temporary residency and work permit that allowed me to stay and work in the US and pay my staff and lawyers. I lived with a heavy cloud of terror over my head for those 11 years.

The other big stressor was that I hadn't been able to go to Colombia because of the asylum processing and a lack of money. I didn't get to see my parents or family at all in that time.

Every day, I walked around wondering what my life would be like if they deported me. I thought about accepting the offer from my aunt to live in Canada if I couldn't stay in the US. There were many things that came to mind, and most of them were negative. After I got permanent citizenship, I was able to go back to Colombia. I wanted to see my family again and to find out what it felt like after 11 years.

When I first came to the United States, I didn't talk to my family that much. My father was mad I left, and then I was mad at my parents because they tried to keep my daughter from me. There was even a time when my daughter had an accident while she was still living in Colombia, and my family didn't call me or tell me for several days.

For a long time, I wasn't speaking to them regularly because the relationship was still rocky.

Then a wise man told me, "If you want to have abundance and prosperity, you have to make your amends with your father. That's why you're not moving forward, Gloria."

When I heard that, I reached out to my father. From there, it was like my life took off again. My feelings toward my family started to change, though things remained rocky for a while and it took me a long time to understand how my own behavior impacted my relationship with my parents.

I traveled to Colombia to see my parents had not changed, but they had gotten divorced.

My father was completely different and saw me like a grown, more mature woman. I showed him that I had made a life that worked, and I took care of myself and my daughter.

I didn't need my parents' help anymore to evolve. But from myself, I needed much more.

DARKNESS INTO LIGHT, TRAUMA INTO FORGIVENESS

My relationship with Allen moved very quickly. Again, it was a trauma attachment. Almost instantly, I felt like he was the one, the guy I wanted to be with forever. But that was just my survival mode.

Very early on, I saw some red flags that told me the relationship wouldn't work. But because I was stubborn—and with my trauma attachment and lack of healing after the kidnapping—I looked past the red flags. I was unconscious and numb to life, which is why I was making the wrong decisions over and over.

Those men weren't bad, but they weren't right for me.

I wasn't vibrating in the vibration of love, which means I wasn't loving myself. I wasn't in a place to have a good relationship, no matter who it was with. But because I had Stockholm Syndrome and needed to attach to someone, I kept looking for relationships.

For a long time, I was a manager in a produce company where I made good money. After 18 years as a quality control inspector and a year as a secretary for a Peruvian company, I knew what I needed to know to start my own business.

An asparagus Peruvian wholesale company was where I learned about accounting early in my career, and it was the first time I realized I wanted to do more with my life than work for someone else. I tried speaking to the company owner to tell him I could do more than be a secretary. I also alerted him to the fact that people were stealing money from him. He didn't believe me and didn't think I could do what I knew I could do. Immediately, I quit.

After I quit this Peruvian company, a Brazilian ginger wholesale company offer me the position of a general manager in the USA, where I had the opportunity to grow to the level of CEO. I worked for them for two years, and I grew so much as a professional and made more and more connections. It was not exactly what I wanted but very close to being a business owner.

Two years later, I meet the owner of the Peruvian company and he said, "Oh, why didn't I listen to you? You could do so much more than what I was having you do. A couple of months after you left, I went into bankruptcy."

It was the confirmation and validation I needed that I was living in alignment, and I was on the right path for myself.

How quickly things can change.

It took a couple of years, but I finally convinced my then-husband Allen to start a business with me.

We began an import and wholesale company, bringing produce into the US from South and Central America and selling it wholesale to other distributors. I helped him build the company, and we made really, really good money.

My main role in the business was to manage the finances. For two years, we worked day and night to build something amazing. I put my heart and soul into the company.

During our third year in business, my husband came to me and said, "I don't want to work with you anymore."

I was heartbroken.

I didn't understand what he was saying. I was the entrepreneur behind the business and helped create the company. I felt degraded and humiliated.

It reminded me of a time when I was younger and I told my father I wanted to be an actress. I always wanted to be in the school plays, and acting was a serious passion of mine. I even had the chance to become a professional actress, but my father wouldn't let me.

He laughed. "You, be an actress? You can't be an actress. You don't have what you need to be an actress."

It was the same feeling of having my dreams dashed and my wings clipped.

When my husband Allen told me he couldn't work with me, he said it was because I was so strong and I get defensive. I worked with a lot of men, and I was very disciplined, strict, and abrasive. Sometimes, I felt I had to be that way so the men would respect me.

Again, I suffered depression. For five weeks, I didn't want to get out of bed. I cried a lot and didn't care about my life or my work.

It was the same self-isolation I resorted to when I was triggered. When I came out of the depression, I was angry.

During my depression, I stumbled across a YouTube video of an artist using paint markers. I bought the same markers and special paper. It wasn't that expensive, which I liked, and I began painting to see what came out. Art became a therapeutic, expressive tool for me to help make sense of my thoughts and emotions.

I even told Allen I wanted to get a divorce as a way of trying to reclaim some of my own personal power. When I had asked him for a divorce the first time, we separated for a little while, but he came back to me and told me he didn't want a divorce. He said he'd change and convinced me that we still belonged together.

My Stockholm Syndrome told me to trust him and that I needed him, but I confused his saying that he would change with his actually changing.

We ended up having a massive problem in our relationship.

Allen and I went to couples therapy for six years. I couldn't believe that he couldn't work with me and that he kicked me out of the company. It took many years and many therapy sessions for me to understand it. I lost trust in him and in myself.

Even though I was going through another traumatic, difficult time, it opened the door for healing and more self-discovery.

The voice in my head said, *Gloria, what are you going to do? You've put 10 years into this relationship, and you aren't working right now. You have everything you could need and don't have to worry about anything in life.*

In therapy, my husband told me it was a struggle for him to see the "good" part of me. I felt like I was constantly trying to prove myself and my worth to him.

One of the problems I had was that I hadn't faced my trauma, so every time I got criticized, I would pout and pout. I would feel sorry for myself and ask, "Why does this keep happening to me?"

I couldn't see that I was attracting the same situations. I was in a lower vibration, and I attracted lower vibration situations. All of these situations let me see my darkness and my shadows so I could start changing my vibration.

Looking back, every one of my relationships provided me with a teacher or master that brought me a lesson. I learned things about myself from each of those relationships, even if I didn't recognize it at the time.

I didn't understand the messages because I wasn't conscious, or aware, that I was getting them. I stayed in that relationship even though I was very, very unhappy. I woke up late every day and spent a lot of money. I felt like my husband had taken away my dream.

I had everything I wanted, but I wasn't happy. Except I didn't have anything. I didn't have freedom to express myself freely, self-love, or a good relationship with people. I realized I had to have a good relationship with myself before I could have a better relationship with people.

How could I ask the world to give me anything if I wasn't going to give back to the world? For years, I kept blaming other people. It was time to take responsibility.

I was looking for healing, a direction, and a purpose. I wanted to help others, heal others, and that led me to massage therapy. It was very holistic and connected me with the other students in my class.

While I was studying massage, one of my teachers discovered something. Every time my teacher came next to me to teach me massage, I would hold my breath.

"Why are you holding your breath when I come to say something to you?" he asked.

"Because I have trust issues," I said, identifying the problem.

Through massage, my teacher helped me work on those trust issues.

Another woman and I clicked right away. We talked a lot, and she knew my story. She told me about a retreat that changed her life and told me to go. She said it could change a lot for me. The retreat was about forgiveness.

Since I didn't know what was wrong with me, I decided to go. It couldn't hurt, and I was hungry for a change. That retreat was like a quantum leap for me. I spent four days in Miami and did very, very deep work where I cried like a baby. It opened my consciousness to who I was and what I was doing. I learned I had been through a lot, and I needed to take care of myself and be gentle with myself.

I began exploring what I really wanted to do. How I wanted to give back to the world and what I could do to help other people.

It took me a long time to realize I was good at whatever I did. Even though my husband had kicked me out of our company, I had been really good there, too.

In massage school, out of the 30 massage students in the class, I was the third best in the entire group.

When I studied to be a yoga teacher, I was one of the best yoga teachers in the group.

When I studied podcasting, I was the number 1 podcaster out of 100 students when I graduated.

I felt like I was regaining parts of myself that had been lost over the years. I was finally healing and working through my trauma.

It wasn't enough, though. I really wanted to talk about my kidnapping and my PTSD. Now that I had words for those feelings, I wanted to share them so that other people might not have to suffer in silence for so long.

Podcasting appealed to me because it allowed me to talk freely without anyone seeing my face. One day, I saw Brian Rose from the digital platform London Real in England. He was huge in the podcasting industry. I signed up with his program. I didn't care how much it cost or what I'd have to do. I wanted to learn how to talk about my experience in a way that would inspire and help others.

I saw it as a continuation of my own healing journey and a way to reach others going through trauma so that I could help them heal, too. They sent me a coach to help me feel relaxed and talk in the podcast about my story. At first, I was nervous. I spoke about things I never told anyone before. I felt exposed, even though my audience couldn't see my face. It was very raw and made me feel vulnerable. But the more I talked about it, the more confidence I gained.

Going through the podcasting course helped me break out of my shell and get more comfortable sharing my story and talking about trauma and mental health. It was rewarding for me, and the people who heard my story told me they also felt inspired. They thought I was crazy because I was going to talk about depression, anxiety, and PTSD. I wanted to be a pioneer in the field. No one was talking about it openly in podcasts at the time.

When I was about to graduate from the course, I said to my coach, Kia Baker, "Let's do a live show to practice what we know." She immediately agreed and we felt amazing doing it. We talked about the veterans because it was Veteran's Day. Kia pushed me to tell my story on a podcast when I was afraid to do it. She is key to helping me tell my story, too.

I also studied to be a public speaker because one of my dreams is to do a TED talk.

So many opportunities are possible for me now that I am living my truth and helping other people recover from trauma and find ways to forgive themselves and others so that they can move on. In fact, it took me a long time to realize that I had to forgive my parents in order to live my own best life.

The way my parents raised me was to always be polite and grateful with people around me.

I realized that in order to repair my relationship with my parents, I needed to start treating them with gratitude and forgiveness if I wanted things to change. I became conscious that some of my actions had broken their hearts, such as when I moved out of the country.

Once I could see that, I started to forgive them because I could understand them better. I also understand that my family had experienced their own fear and trauma around my kidnapping.

I didn't know until many years later that my parents refused to pay the ransom at first to stall the kidnappers. The entire time, they were working to save me.

Recently, I asked my father about the time he told me I didn't look like I'd been kidnapped because I looked too healthy. He told me he didn't remember saying that to me, and if he said it, it came from a place of concern. Because everything happened so fast, he said he didn't have time to think about his words.

He also told me that my mother had to take medication for her to be able to talk to me on the radio when I was a hostage. I didn't know that at the time, but it has also helped me move forward in forgiving them.

You may not know what is happening with someone that could be driving their actions. Be conscious that what you see might not be the whole story.

It's been decades since I was kidnapped, and I finally feel my energy changing. I feel younger and more vibrant. The first 50 years of my life were very hard, but I'm going forward living with passion and calm.

CONCLUSION

Writing this book has been an important part of my healing process. It took me almost 17 years to embrace my truth and tell my story. It's been a very challenging path, but I would not change any of it because I gained an abundance of wisdom. You need to live life to receive its knowledge.

I wrote this book to help people who feel they are in a dark place, like I was many times. Now, I comprehend life much better and am very happy to be here on this planet. It took me a long time to understand why I had the kidnapping experience and find a way to process it and share it with the world.

Mine is just one of many stories that can help you understand Stockholm Syndrome and all the emotions that trauma can evoke. You don't need to be kidnapped to get stuck in survival mode.

I want this book to open your mind and give you the strength and reflective ability to change if you feel trapped by your relationship, job, family, or anything else in your life. I want you to open yourself to transformation and allow yourself to let go of trauma to live an extraordinary life.

I've never regretted forgiving my parents. It felt like the right thing to do, but it has been a journey. My true healing didn't begin until I found my purpose.

My mission is to help you activate yourself for a better life. Times goes so fast that you risk missing the miracles and beautiful opportunities life presents. This book is just one of many ways I share my experiences and the wisdom I've gained.

I share this story with love for you. Don't be afraid to share your truth, and don't let too much time go by before you learn to love yourself and live your best life.

I have an extraordinary life! What about YOU?

ADDITIONAL RESOURCES

Bourbeau, L. (2021). *Las 5 heridas que impiden ser uno mismo.* Planeta Publishing.

Branden, N. (1995). *The Six Pillars of Self-Esteem.* Bantam.

Byrne, L. (2011). *Angels in My Hair: The True Story of a Modern-Day Irish Mystic.* Harmony.

Bryne, R. (2020). *The Greatest Secret.* HarperOne.

Chiles, N., Storey, T. (2021). *The Miracle Mentality: Tap into the Source of Magical Transformation in Your Life.* Harper Horizon.

Chopra, D. (2011). *The Secret of Love: Meditations for Attracting and Being in Love.* Audible

Coelho, P. (2018). *El Don Supremo [The Supreme Gift].* Sant Jordi Asociados.

Dispenza, J. (2019). *Becoming Supernatural: How Common People are Doing the Uncommon.* Hay House Inc.

Dispenza, J. (2017). *Evolve Your Brain: The Science of Changing Your Mind.* Tantor Audio.

Evans, P. (2015). *The Verbally Abusive Relationship: How to Recognize It and How to Respond.* Adams Media.

Fox, E. (2013). *The 7 Day Mental Diet: How to Change Your Life in a Week.* Merchant Books.

Frank, V. E. (2015). *El hombre en busca de sentido.* Herder Editorial.

Gawain, S. (1999). *Creative Visualization Meditations.* New World Library Audible.

Graziosi, D. (2019). *Millionaire Success Habits: The Gateway to Wealth & Prosperity.* Hay House Inc.

Hawkins, D.R. (2019). *Dejar ir [Letting Go]: El camino de la Liberación [The Path of Liberation].* El Grano de Mostaza. Audible

Hill, N. (2008). *The Law of Success: The Master Wealth-Builder's Complete and Original Lesson Plan for Achieving Your Dreams.* Tarcher Perigee.

Hill, N. (2020). *Think and Grow Rich!* Sound Wisdom. Audible

Honda, K. (2019). *Happy Money: The Japanese Art of Making Peace with Your Money.* Simon & Schuster Audio. Audible

Jordorowsky, A. (2005). *Psicomagia.* Debolsillo.

Kimsey-House, H. et al. (2018). *Co-Active Coaching.* Nicholas Brealey.

Labossier, S. (2017). *The Man God Has For You: 7 traits to Help You Determine Your Life Partner.* Highly Favored Publishing.

Levine, A. and Heller, R. (2012). *Attached: The New Science of Adult Attachment and How It Can Help You Find - and Keep - Love.* TarcherPerigee.

Manson, M. (2014). *El sutil arte de que te importe un caraj*: Un enfoque disruptivo para vivir una buena vida.* 2nd Edition. HarperCollins Mexico.

Myss, C. (2003). *Sacred Contracts: Awakening Your Divine Potential*. Harmony.

Redfield, J. (2018). *Las nueve revelaciones*. Vergara.

Rey, A. *Curación Empática (Empath Healing): Evita el Abuso Narcisista y Comienza a ser más Sensible, Mejorando tus Habilidades Psíticas Empáticas como la... de Aura y la Telepatía*. Gold Inc. Ltd.

Ruiz, D.M. (1999). *Los cuatro acuerdos: una guía práctica para la libertad personal*. Amber-Allen Publishing.

Sadhguru. (2016). *Inner Engineering: A Yogi's Guide to Joy*. Spiegel & Grau.

Sarno, J.E. (2018). *Healing Back Pain: The Mind-Body Connection*. Grand Central.

Schwartz, R. (2012). *Your Soul's Gift: The Healing Power of the Life You Planned Before You Were Born*. Whispering Winds Press.

Silver, T. (2018). *Change Me Prayers: The Hidden Power of Spiritual Surrender*. Atria Books.

Silver, T. (2020). *It's Not Your Money: How to Live Fully from Divine Abundance*. Hay House Inc.

Silver, T. (2016). *Outrageous Openness: Letting the Divine Take the Lead*. Atria Books.

Singer, M. (2015). *The Surrender Experiment: My Journey into Life's Perfection*. Harmony/Rodale.

St. John of the Cross. (2003). *Dark Night of the Soul*. Dover Publications.

Tolle, E. (2004). *The Power of Now: A Guide to Spiritual Enlightenment*. New World Library.

Vernick, L. (2013). *The Emotionally Destructive Marriage: How to Find Your Voice and Reclaim Your Hope*. WaterBrook.

Williams, J. W. (2019). *Inteligencia Emocional: La transformación mental de 21 días para dominar sus emociones, mejorar sus habilidades sociales y lograr mejores y más... Emocional Práctica.* Independently published.

Wolynn, M. (2016). *It Didn't Start with You: How Inherited Family Trauma Shapes Who We Are and How to End the Cycle.* Penguin Audio. Audible

Dedication to My Grandfather Benjamin that
before he pass away push me in to write this book,
He said mija don't be afraid! just do it.

Thank you Granpa